"This personal witty and insightful book teaches us about the fears that drive failure and the navigate it. The great point abe philosophical with regards the achievement, and practical. Fo a fear of failure, it offers a way t
Luke Johnson, serial entrepreneur, *Financial Times* columnist and Chairman of the *RSA*

"This powerful, insightful book shows you how to unlock your unconscious brakes and step on the accelerator of your true potential!"
Brian Tracy, author of *Maximum Achievement, Goals!* and *Eat That Frog*

"This is a must-read book for anyone concerned with achieving long-term professional success. Not only does Kelsey explain our common insecurities in the most readable and entertaining ways, he delivers strategies and tactics that really work."
Martin Yate CPC, *NY Times* bestseller of the *Knock 'em Dead* series of books including *Knock 'em Dead: The Ultimate Job Search Guide*

"Robert Kelsey has combined thorough research, careful thought and the lessons of his own experience to produce a valuable, original and eminently readable book. I can strongly recommend it to anyone whose progress has been impeded by fear of failure."
John Caunt, author of *Boost Your Self-esteem*

"Why do talented people sabotage their own chances of success? Often the answer is that they are afraid of failure. Kelsey provides a practical guide for overcoming this common problem. Clear, engaging, and to the point."
Dylan Evans, author of *Emotion: The Science of Sentiment*

What's Stopping You?

Why Smart People Don't Always Reach Their Potential, and How You Can

Robert Kelsey

CAPSTONE

Library of Congress Cataloguing-in-Publication Data

9780857081728 (paperback), ISBN 9780857081803 (epub), 9780857081810 (emobi), ISBN 9780857081827 (epdf)

A catalogue record for this book is available from the British Library.

Set in 10/13.5 pt Sabon by Toppan Best-set Premedia Limited
Printed and Bound in the United Kingdom by TJ International, Padstow, Cornwall.

CONTENTS

FOREWORD BY LUKE JOHNSON

Most of us know that the secret to success is confidence. Good looks, intelligence, qualifications – all these help, but with many of the highest achievers I've met, their greatest asset has been their world class chutzpah.

Unfortunately, many of us don't possess such bountiful self-assurance. We are racked with doubts. We focus too much on the losing shots, not our aces. So Robert Kelsey has written a book for the rest of us, everyone who lacks confidence, who can be too self-critical, who isn't sure if they're up to it or going to make it. And I think it's a winner.

The truth is that such feelings are self-fulfilling. Just as the confident person creates the mental conditions for their own success, the person that lacks confidence – or that fears failure – is creating the mental conditions for their lack of progress. This makes fear of failure a debilitating condition but also one where improvement is possible, not least because failure is the very thing that confident people don't fear. As Robert Kelsey proves, the ability to fall flat on your face without it undermining your desire to keep trying is perhaps the most important quality those high-chutzpah types possess.

Certainly, success is not about being ambitious – that's easy. It's about overcoming adversity. And in my experience what separates the winners and the losers in life is how they handle disappointment. Achievement in any field is impossible without setbacks.

What separates the field is not the setback, however, but the response to it.

This book offers help to those that, up until now, have been stymied by setbacks – indeed, may have even avoided participation for fear of encountering a setback. Yet the great point about this book is that it is both philosophical with regards the nature of fear and its impact on achievement, and practical. For those that may be paralyzed by a fear of failure, it offers a way through – not through the impractical dream-fulfilment nonsense of many self-help books but through step-by-step advice on the fears that attack us at each stage, and why and how we can think and act differently for a better outcome.

The author has not invented a new philosophy or programme for living. Rather he has summarized the contents of scores of relevant self-help books – picking the bits that work, ignoring the bits that don't. His aim is to create a tailored route for those that may simply be trying to avoid failure – helping them get a better result than they are currently experiencing. There are, after all, reams of such volumes in print. And while some are useful, many of them are not. The author has covered the waterfront, and has selected the most practical and reliable advice from his research of hundreds of psychologists, therapists and self-help gurus.

What's Stopping You? is also a highly personal book. The author talks in depth about his own career journey, how he overcame his own demons by studying the literature, by really analysing his own issues, and by developing techniques to deal with them. Sometimes amusing, sometimes cringing, sometimes painful – his own experiences add to the impression that this is a book written from the heart, even if it is aimed squarely at the head.

Robert Kelsey is a rare beast because he runs his own business – but he can also actually write. He participates and he also reports – and thinks deeply about the challenges. Word processing has enabled everyone to churn out reams of material. But few who tackle these types of subjects actually have any literary ability: in reality their prose style stinks. Now, you might argue that it doesn't matter if modern day writers can't construct decent sentences or mount a sensible argument. But it absolutely does and it absolutely helps with respect to the reader's learning and progress in this instance.

More than anything I enjoyed reading this book. And that makes a difference when so many business and self-help books are bought and never read – partly because they are essentially unreadable. But Mr Kelsey's text is highly enjoyable and eminently fluent. Moreover, it is a book that doesn't have to be read like a novel. It can be used for reference purposes: kept and dipped in when needed, with checklists and bullet points and plenty of down to earth stuff about how best to effect change and follow through for a better result. In this respect the book is well targeted – addressing mere mortals with ordinary hopes and fears, not the fantasy superheroes that many self-help writers are expecting the reader to become after just a few short chapters.

Not all the tips here will work for everyone. But there is a sufficient range of topics for any reader – and especially any reader that has suffered from a debilitating lack of confidence – to find something relevant to their situation: from goal setting to handling work colleagues, from discovering your true values and motivations to starting a business.

What's Stopping You? is an honest, thoughtful guide to the jungle of career and business fulfilment. Kelsey doesn't promise the earth, and is endearingly open about his own ups and downs. He is grounded but he isn't cynical. This is not a book about impossible, and perhaps unsustainable, dream fulfilment. It is a book for the expedient – those wishing to make progress by ridding themselves of the very fears that destroy their potential for progress.

So I wholeheartedly endorse this book, and encourage the casual reader to put it on their bedside table and browse it at regular intervals: for inspiration, for understanding, and for pragmatic advice. I've enjoyed reading it, and I think you will too.

Luke Johnson
Chairman of Risk Capital Partners
and the Royal Society for the Encouragement of
Arts, Manufactures and Commerce

INTRODUCTION

"Failure is not an option," said the actor playing Gene Kranz, flight director for Mission Control in *Apollo 13*, the 1995 movie dramatizing the near-disaster of the third Apollo mission to the Moon. But he was wrong. It *was* an option, which is why he said it. Kranz was employing classic alpha-male posturing to implore his team to lose their *fear of failure*.

He knew that failure was staring them in the face but, given the consequences of failure, any other option was not only preferable but imperative. Had he said "failure is almost certain, but let's have a go anyway" his team would have remained focused on their personal fears, as well as the potential humiliation of suggesting a daft idea. Yet daft ideas were the only thing that could save the astronauts, so Kranz had to find a way of getting them on the table – hence upping the stakes in order to overcome his team's individual fears.

Fear of failure

Yet *Apollo 13* is a movie and those words were written by a scriptwriter (despite the real Gene Kranz later adopting them for the title of his biography). The fears that prevent us from achieving our goals are usually mundane, private, nuanced and sometimes so subtle that many of us may not fully accept their impact on our thoughts and actions.

As Kranz well knew, fear of failure changes our behaviour in ways that render failure a near certainty. Fear paralyses our decision-making, throws our judgement and destroys our creativity. Yet as mental conditions go, fear of failure is not only one of the most common – with millions of sufferers in the UK alone – it is also one of the least acknowledged or acted upon, partly because those with the condition are so paralyzed by their fear of humiliation or public embarrassment they suffer in silence, or even in self-denial, rather than seek treatment.

They are chained to the seabed, unable to swim towards the sunlight above due to their fears and insecurities. Of course, some may express their fears through depression or anger without even realizing what lies behind such symptoms – making them hostage to behaviour that further confirms their inner fears and further destroys their potential for progress.

And while the actor playing Kranz unlocked the potential of his team with one powerful phrase, we are unlikely to be so lucky. Even if we acknowledge our fears and seek to overcome them we may find ourselves bewildered by the hundreds of self-help books offering more confidence, higher self-esteem, greater success and even "unlimited power". Some deal directly with fear of failure. Others focus on related or underlying conditions such as lack of confidence or low self-esteem. Many offer a near-instant cure – the banishment of our frailties and the certainty of success – through a mental realignment injected into us via some, admittedly strong, motivational words and techniques.

But a health warning is required. Promising the chance to be born again as a new, more confident, even fearless person is a false promise made to the afflicted desperate for a cure. Conditions such as fear of failure – as well as antecedents such as low self-esteem – are, as we shall see, innate. Once and however inflicted they are here to stay.

That's the bad news. The good news is that we can accept this and make strong progress anyway. In fact, in my opinion strong sustainable progress is *only* possible once we have accepted that our fears and primary beliefs are here to stay. We *can* learn to live with who we are – including our insecurities. We don't have to banish them forever in order to move forward. We *can* achieve our goals. As long as they are the right goals, *our* goals – not false goals potentially fed to us by external influences or our own faulty thinking.

And that's where this book comes in. People with a fear of failure need a map. This book is not a map. In fact, we have to draw our own map and even that will require many redrafts before being even vaguely accurate. What this book provides, I hope, is guidance on how to go about drawing such a map: in draft, fuzzy at the edges, containing plenty of "here be dragons" elements, but a map nonetheless. Something we can grasp and regard as we cut through the thicket. Something that allows us to take those all-important next steps.

The monkey on my back

I have suffered from a debilitating fear of failure all my life – itself the result of poor confidence brought about by a low self-esteem developed in early childhood. At key moments in my life fear has led me to doubt my abilities to succeed, which has profoundly changed my behaviour in ways that made success less likely: often snatching a humiliating defeat from the jaws of victory. And I have read scores of books in an effort to shift what I call the "monkey on my back" – the creature that whispers fear and self-doubt in my ear at critical moments.

But the monkey hasn't disappeared. He just wouldn't go away, which didn't seem to compute with the literature I was reading, much of which promised both a cure for my insecurities and the certainty of dream fulfilment. Clearly, I was doing something wrong: perhaps not applying the methodology diligently enough or maintaining destructive behaviours and beliefs. Yet I now realize it was their prognosis that was flawed because it took too little account of the fact I am who I am, and that monkey comes too.

Surely a more powerful book would describe a route towards progress from our own flawed perspective – answering the question "what's stopping you?" with the answer: you are (and the monkey, of course). Yet it would also state that we must accept the monkey as a fellow passenger and plan to make progress anyway. It would spot and describe the likely barriers preventing progress, as well as the false assumptions they may generate.

Certainly, if we could see that it was our responses to those barriers that were producing the poor results, not the barriers themselves – nor was it poor luck, innate ineptitude or even prejudice against us – then we may be able to generate better results.

We don't need a miracle cure injected into us. We just need to take account of our insecurities and navigate our way forward accordingly.

A practitioner in failure

I am a practitioner in failure with a childhood and early adulthood punctuated with one self-fulfilling educational and career disaster after another.

Written-off as stupid by low-grade junior-school teachers, and traumatized by the immediately-preceding break-up of my family, I failed the 11-plus, ended up in the local secondary-modern turned comprehensive and left school at 15 with one 'O' level. I was taken on by a local building surveyor who needed someone to hold a stripy pole in muddy fields, although he kindly enrolled me on a day-a-week diploma course. Inevitably, I bunked the course – instead spending the days walking the streets of London with a day-return ticket in my pocket.

This eventually landed me a job looking after the vast residential property portfolio of the London region's gas board. I was 18 at the time and loved it. I was working for a large West End surveying firm full of graduates and professionals. They were nice to me despite my gruff accent and manners, and encouraged me to return to education. So, realizing I was as capable as them, I enrolled on an evening 'A' level course and, five years later, graduated from the University of Manchester with a high 2:1 joint-honours degrees in Politics & Modern History.

I had no career plan other than a vague notion of going into journalism, which – after a few false turns – led to my becoming a staff-writer then editor for a banking-focused magazine, and eventually also to becoming a banker in what the City describes as a "gamekeeper turned poacher move".

As I relate in Part One, I was not a great banker. Paralysed by fear, I worked in both London and the US before realizing I was simply not cut out for finance. Once again without a plan, I was recruited by a friend with a plan – for a dotcom "incubator" (this was around the turn of the millennium) – and together we founded Metrocube, an "e-business community" that incubated over 200 companies before being sold a few years after the dotcom crash.

Cured of my journalistic and banking ambitions, and somewhat bitten by the entrepreneurial bug, I then combined my experiences and started Moorgate Communications, a financial public relations agency aimed at banks, which has been a sustainable and fulfilling enterprise – even growing through the financial meltdown of 2008–09.

And I wrote a book on my banking experiences in New York, which was published in 2000 and had me all set – I thought – for a career as a humorous, laddish writer in the Nick Hornby or Michael Lewis mould. However, the book sold less than I'd hoped and my dream was dashed.

An addiction to self-help

The book-writing career aside, it is possible to read the above and think I am, in fact, a long way from being a practitioner in failure.

But that's because I have edited out the fears, frustrations, moods, paranoia, anguish and temper tantrums that have punctuated every one of the above experiences. Terrorized by my own insecurities, I have been a nightmare to work with and apologize now to any colleagues that had to suffer my nonsense.

But I have also made considerable progress in facing up to my fears and insecurities. Perhaps surprisingly, given my earlier comments, much of this has been due to my ongoing addiction to self-help books. This began while in the US – where the acres of shelves dedicated to the genre suggest an openness that the UK is only slowly adopting – although it took a deeper hold of me back in the UK as I began to realize the problem was not a particular job or person or set of circumstances. The problem was me.

Ultimately, and as described within, this landed me in the hands of a professional psychologist. Yet far from complementing the work of all those self-help gurus, the shrink – plus further research of my own – opened my eyes to the gaping hole between what the psychologists state about our innate (but treatable) personalities and the near-instant and life-changing promises and cures on offer from the self-help gurus.

My first reaction to this was – not untypically – anger. The gurus seemed to be offering false hope and unrealistic dreams that could ultimately leave people further weakened. But then the penny dropped. Much of what they convey has been incredibly useful. Their tips and techniques can be both logical and inspiring. Someone rejecting their divinity with respect to the earthly paradise promised can, therefore, still make use of their, often very practical, advice and methodologies – many of which pepper the pages ahead.

Certainly I still fight the fear every day, as well as my low self-esteem. But I now realize this is part of my chemistry and that such a chemistry doesn't condemn me. It just means I must take it into account. And it is both the flawed thinking and behaviour of those with a high fear of failure – as well as related insecurities such as low self-esteem – and the progress possible despite it, that I wish to convey in this book.

What's Stopping You? *Your insecurities are part of your chemistry. They cannot be removed through instant cures. Yet strong progress is possible once you realize who you are and take this into account.*

PART ONE

What *is* Stopping You?

1

FEAR

Ask what was stopping *me* and I can tell you immediately: fear. Fear of failure, in fact. Relationship issues with parents, siblings, teachers and peers can be a cause, as can other traumatic events in childhood – especially ones where we feel demeaned or humiliated. But the fear can build from tiny beginnings into an uncontrollable phobia that can mentally paralyse the sufferer in adulthood. It can also strike us at various stages in our career – even once we are seemingly beyond it or have built up strong confidence in a particular area.

My disastrous investment banking "career" provides a strong example in my own story. A seemingly-confident financial journalist with a strong and detailed knowledge of corporate banking, I caught the eye of a leading corporate bank and, after a protracted interview and assessment process, persuaded them I had the perfect training and background for joining their growing corporate banking team within the investment bank.

Yet once inside the door my behaviour changed. I became fearful that my knowledge was paper-thin and I possessed nothing more than a talent for empty bravado. Of course, this was probably true, but was no different to the majority of bankers in the room – all with very narrow experience compared to my breadth and strength of knowledge across the corporate banking spectrum (exactly the knowledge required for a corporate banking salesperson, in fact). But having sold myself well during the recruitment process, once a practising banker I became scared of putting a foot wrong – leaving them wondering what had happened to the confident, even cocky, person they'd employed as their next hotshot "originator".

My role was to originate US$100 million-plus financings for the bank to arrange and distribute to investors. These looked easy when writing about them. I thought we just found a willing borrower, asked for some security (we were looking for trade receivables such as oil shipments), handed over the money and waited for it to come back with interest. But half the banks in London were doing the same, forcing me into one of the scariest margins of the 1990s corporate borrower universe: Russia.

In the mid-1990s businessmen were being gunned down on a daily basis on the streets of Moscow, and my clients – the newly-privatized Russian oil companies – were certainly menacing organizations to deal with. Yet that wasn't the bit that scared me. In fact, that helped mask my real terror, which was the bank discovering how little I knew about how to structure one of these deals. I couldn't calculate the volumes of oil required to repay the loan, or establish what volumes had to be where, when, and how they got there. It looked way too complex for my simple brain.

And the fact no one in the bank had this knowledge – we simply took the information on trust from the oil companies – didn't seem to bother anyone but me, which was a key part of the problem with my banking career. Taking such risks is the nuts and bolts of banking. Yet I couldn't help visualizing one of about 20 disaster scenarios being played out in various hostile environments somewhere out there in the post-Soviet steppes – all of which would have rendered my banking career over in a puff of public humiliation.

Blind to office politics

Being risk-averse and technically inept should not have meant curtains for my banking career, however. Fear stalked the corridors of the entire bank – as did technical ineptitude, come to that. The ultimate reason for failing as an investment banker was that all those technically-inept and risk-averse bankers prospered by being hotshots at office politics. They had strong judgement regarding where the bank was heading and could make self-enhancing decisions on that basis.

But I was awful at office politics. And I had terrible judgement – based on trying to hide my fears and insecurities rather than focusing on the interests of the bank (or myself) – which led me to trust the wrong people and back the wrong deals. My behaviour changed to the point where I came across as a fool, and soon started being treated as one. Any deal on my desk looked dodgy for the simple reason it was on my desk, and any new project that came my way soon acquired a distinctly hot-potato feel to it.

Even the transfer to America – sold to me as the "move that could make you" – was no more than turning-out-the-lights on a failing office. The only way I could make it work was by discovering the one entity that would hoover up our loan structures no matter what: Enron.

Yet rather than focus on the skills required to become a competent banker – especially the soft skills such as calculating who could and couldn't be trusted and recruiting people to my cause – I soon sought a way out of banking. I fell back on my core skill of journalism and started writing about my life in New York, which before long had a greater hold on my imagination, and time, than a banking career that I was rejecting, seemingly before it could reject me.

Emotions and their role in survival

I detail the fears and behaviour that destroyed my banking career because they seem odd given that it took some guts to win the job in the first place and that I had obviously been judged as having the required knowledge and at least the capabilities of learning the trade by those within the bank. Yet, as we shall see, those suffering from fear of failure are often able to take extreme risks in situations where failure is almost certain, while finding themselves paralysed by everyday situations that involve only moderate but often very public risks. And they are more than capable of changing their behaviour in ways that make failure more likely – all of which makes fear of failure a debilitating and self-fulfilling condition seemingly at odds with today's career needs.

So how did we get to the point where so many people sabotage their own advancement through such self-harming behaviour? In his book *Emotion: The Science of Sentiment* (2001), British philosopher Dylan Evans tackles this conundrum by asking the question that, given the fact emotions such as fear and sadness seem to be "hardwired" into humans: why are they so bad for modern careers? Or looking at it the other way: as such emotions seem to offer no economic advantage – in fact, just the opposite – why have they not died out in the process of natural selection?

He wonders why we have not evolved to behave like Spock in *Star Trek* and judge life's trials in purely logical terms. The conclusion appears to be that Spock's home planet of Vulcan was entirely free of predators. Meanwhile on Earth, Evans contests that emotions evolved as a quick-reflexive action aimed at encouraging survival – hence it often arriving as an uncontrollable nerve-surge through the body.

Joy, distress, fear, anger, disgust: all played a key role in helping our survival in the State of Nature, says Evans. And to an extent we rarely acknowledge, such emotions continue to play an important evaluation role today, just a more subtle one. Evans provides evidence of this by observing those unable to use their emotions for evaluation.

"Those that lose their emotional capacity through brain damage tend to be easy victims for the unscrupulous," he observes. "Forced to rely on their logical reasoning, they make disastrous choices about whom they can trust."

Impaired mental capacity

Evans makes an important point because, as we shall see, those of us with fear of failure may well have such fears due to an impaired mental capacity when it comes to reasoning and evaluations – perhaps due to poor conditioning or traumatic events as a child – meaning that we are also vulnerable, with fear being our response to that vulnerability. So emotions remain important in the modern world, which means that an impaired capacity to use our emotions to evaluate situations is potentially disastrous – or at best paralysing.

Does this therefore enslave us to the potency of our emotions, forcing those with impaired evaluations into self-destructive behaviour? Not always. Plenty of people behave in ways not dictated by their emotions. The stiff upper lip of the English upper classes is no myth, but is an external response rather than inward feeling – a training from an early age to hide emotions rather than change them – not dissimilar to the poker face of the professional gambler who may inwardly be in emotional turmoil. Indeed, such responses are only ever a mask. In reality "quiet desperation is the English way" – at least according to *Pink Floyd*.

Such masking takes training and is, in any case, an unsatisfactory response in the modern world where we are encouraged to express ourselves, or at least to behave in ways that generate trust and understanding rather than distrust and misunderstanding. And such a masking may simply delay a terrible reckoning – a breakdown as the mask slips and then collapses due to the pressure. Far better, surely, to try and understand our emotions, as well as how emotions such as fear can motivate and demotivate us, and how they can impair our evaluations and change our behaviours. Surely self-awareness trumps self-denial every time?

Experiments in emotional manipulation

In his book *Motivation* (1975) psychologist Phil Evans details the relatively short history of academic experiments on our emotions – and particularly on fear – and how they impact our motivation.

For instance, in 1948 the pioneering American psychologist Neal Miller experimented on the impact of fear on behaviour by placing rats in a box with two compartments – one black, one white – with those in the white zone consistently given electric shocks. Of course, the rats soon exhibited great reluctance to venture into the white zone, even overcoming physical barriers in order to escape to the safety of the black zone. And before long, Miller's harassed rodents needed only to catch sight of the white zone to exhibit signs of stress. Miller concluded that fear as a driver can be quickly acquired, can change behaviour profoundly, and can internally condition the rat to elicit a fear response when subsequently triggered (i.e. when reminded of the trauma).

Unsurprisingly, such emotional conditioning is also applicable with humans, at even a subtle level. Evans cites Judson S. Brown, a post-war American psychologist who thought that, due to fear, humans spend much of their time in search of "reinforcers" such as money and in performing "operant responses" such as holding down a job. Brown's thesis was that what a person was seeking was potentially less important than what a person was avoiding. A person could be said to be making money, he considered, but could equally be motivated by the fear of *not* making money.

For me, Brown's focus on avoidance is beginning to get to the heart of the matter with respect to fear as a driver. Yet it is Stanford University's John W. Atkinson's work on "achievement motivation" (which he and others shortened to "nAch" – meaning "need for achievement" – although I think "AM" may be easier to remember) that really roots out the key issues with respect to fear of failure.

Again, detailed by Evans, Atkinson (with G.H. Litwin – and following on from experiments by David McClelland) set groups of children achievement-related tasks and noticed that they approached them in one of two ways: anticipating success or anticipating failure. Atkinson concluded that an individual's performance was dictated by whether they had high or low levels of innate "achievement motivation" – with those with high AM levels driven by their expectations regarding the payoff of task fulfilment, and those with low AM levels motivated to avoid the task due to an anticipation, or fear, of failure (which he shortened to FF).

Left to choose their tasks, he noticed that those with high achievement motivation ("High-AMs" as we shall call them) chose a middle range of demanding tasks because they were focused on the rewards of success. Meanwhile, those with low AM, or high fear of failure ("High-FFs" as we shall call them) became anxious about even intermediately-difficult tasks and, in many cases, sought to avoid the task completely.

Yet Atkinson made one further – extraordinary – discovery. High-FFs had no problem attempting tasks that were deemed very difficult or almost impossible. This was due to the fact the price of failure was reduced. So while High-AMs chose a challenging but achievable range of tasks in anticipation of success and reward, High-FFs chose only those tasks that they were almost certain to complete or almost certain to fail, along with everyone else attempting that task. For instance, Atkinson involved children in a game of throwing hoops on a peg. High-AMs stood a bold but realistic distance from the peg while High-FFs stood either right on top of the peg, or so far back success was almost impossible.

Task perseverance, task avoidance

Australian psychologist Norman Feather undertook similar experiments and came to similar conclusions – finding a bias in the willingness of subjects to persist in a task they had failed first-time based on their levels of achievement motivation. Those with high levels of achievement motivation (our High-AMs) would tend to persevere – perhaps reassessing the difficulty of the task and adding further concentration or determination. Meanwhile, those with a high fear of failure (our High-FFs) were disinclined to continue, wanting to avoid the shame of failing.

Feather also found that he could manipulate the response by presenting the task as easy or difficult. High-FFs were inclined to continue if they were told that the task was difficult because, he concluded, the shame of failing had been lowered. In fact, the task he'd been setting his subjects – drawing around a figure without lifting the pen from the paper – was impossible, although at first glance appeared easy.

Summarising the experiments, Phil Evans contended that levels of achievement motivation played a significant role when it came to "the wisdom of career choices in students". High-AM students would choose realistic but challenging careers – perhaps joining a profession or becoming a scientist. They aimed high – avoiding careers with low incentives – but were grounded. They steered clear of pursuing overly-ambitious or unrealistic "wildest dreams" such as pop stardom or TV fame. High-FFs, on the other hand, would either keep their career choices at an uninspiring level or aim for something that would bring either fabulous rewards (such as fame) or, far more likely, failure – although the consequences of failure would be judged kindly simply because success was so unlikely. Indeed, in these circumstances, being seen as a "trier" would be viewed positively.

Mastery or ego orientation

Phil Evans's excellent recounting of the history of experiments studying the emotional drivers for our behaviour was published in the mid 1970s. Yet the research he detailed is backed up in the 1980s by Carol Dweck and Ellen Leggett. Their goal-setting experiments concluded that children were either "mastery-oriented" or "ego-oriented" with the mastery-oriented kids (High-AMs in other words) believing not only that they could surmount obstacles and reach a solution but relished the opportunity of doing so.

For mastery-oriented kids, learning or skill improvement was their focus, meaning they would persist in the face of setbacks, while ego-oriented kids (i.e. High-FFs) were more inclined towards not losing face, so would avoid situations where this was a possibility. Their need for achievement, it seems, was lower than their need to not appear foolish. Of course, for both groups there were major implications for their future academic and career achievement levels as well as their development of life-long learning habits.

So we seem to have a well-known psychological phenomenon on our hands. High-AMs are not worried about the possibility of failure and tend to be stimulated by situations involving some degree of risk. They are more likely to accept challenges where the probability of success is no more than possible, and perceive easy tasks as too boring or beneath them to attempt. Meanwhile, High-FFs fear public humiliation and therefore seek to avoid the potential for failure. They are more likely to attempt only very simple tasks or tasks that are all but impossible simply because they would win credit for trying and it may mask their avoidance of more attainable goals.

Self-help books aimed at High-FFs

Evans's book was aimed at an academic audience, although it produced a strong personal response in me. Secretly, self-denyingly – but absolutely – I was a High-FF. I feared failure and acted accordingly, whether this was with immediate tasks or life choices. This was true in my careers but had a resonance in every aspect of my life and certainly my academic failures as a child.

Yet Evans's book had been published in 1975 (I'd found my copy in a small-town second-hand bookshop) with the experiments on motivation going back to the 1960s. So why had all the "how to succeed" literature I'd gorged upon over the years not addressed the fundamental issues exposed by the experiments, not least the inappropriate goal-setting of the High-FF?

Indeed, those "how to succeed" books are a major publishing genre occupying miles of shelving (especially in the US). Alain de Botton in *Status Anxiety* (2004) claims they started with Benjamin Franklin's *Autobiography* (1790), which encouraged readers to act through homilies such as "there are no gains without pains" and "early to bed, early to rise . . .".

William Matthews's 1874 book *Getting On in the World* was the first to attack the subject head on, followed by William Maher's *On the Road to Riches* (1876), Edwin T Freedley's *The Secret of Success in Life* (1881), Lyman Abbott's *How to Succeed* (1882) and William Speer's *The Law of Success* (1885). And on and on, through Dale Carnegie's *How to Win Friends and Influence People* (1936), to Napoleon Hill's *Think and Grow Rich* (1937), to Frank Bettger's *How I Raised Myself From Failure to Success in Selling* (1947), to Anthony Robbins *Unlimited Power* (1986) and even to *Winnie the Pooh on Success* by Roger E. Allen and Stephen D. Allen (1997).

Notice anything? Every one of these books is addressing someone with a high fear of failure, yet their key message is that it is OK to reach for the stars. "Go on, you *can* be a popstar," they seem to be saying before imparting admittedly-useful methodologies for goal achievement.

Susan Jeffers in *Feel the Fear and do it Anyway* (1987) at least addresses the core concern. But what if "doing it" wasn't the right thing to do? What if people were setting the wrong goals based on their fear of failure – avoiding, sustainable and obtainable careers in favour of the avoidance-based "wildest dreams" the books seem to encourage? As a High-FF, what I needed from a self-help book was guidance in developing the evaluation and motivation skills of those with high achievement motivation. A book that says: "look, just maybe your entire concept of goal-setting and achievement is flawed and needs rethinking".

Just maybe the answer isn't about "obtaining our highest goal" but about setting goals that are appropriate and lead to fulfilment. Rather than "feeling the fear and doing it anyway" what about recognising that fear may be leading us in the wrong direction?

Dream fulfilment is a false promise

While the AM/FF split is well documented it appears to have been ignored by much of the modern self-help literature, which – while clearly aimed at frustrated people with an acute fear of failure, or with related issues such as poor confidence – perhaps assumes we would retain our unrealistic and avoidance-based goals even if we could overcome our fears. Meanwhile, those boring High-AMs are already grounded and thus an unlikely market for books on self-improvement.

Yet as a saturated High-FF it dawned on me that it was the dream that needed adjusting. The very idea of dream fulfilment is a false promise – potentially even a lie. It is a comfort blanket that, in reality, suffocates personal fulfilment through the idea that it is "all or nothing", so the only high-esteem choice is "all" – the pursuit of which will result in either abject failure or arrogant whooping success that, for insecure High-FFs, generates as many problems as it solves.

Indeed, for the first time I saw celebrity behaviour – the arrogance, the addictions, the inappropriate marriages and affairs, and the wanton self-destruction – as it really is. Many celebrities are High-FFs that by some miracle have hooped the distant peg and are now floundering around in a sea of insecurities. Those with high achievement motivation, meanwhile, are lawyers or accountants or medics or just about anything else that is successful, normal and involves high levels of sustainable self-esteem.

"Attribution theory" and the "locus of control"

But the psychologists weren't finished. In the late 1980s Bernard Weiner, a cognitive psychologist at the University of California, published his "attribution theory" to explain the emotional and motivational aspects of academic success and failure.

From Weiner's work it becomes clear that our frame of mind makes a major difference. Those with a positive frame of mind (our High-AMs) attribute their successes to their own abilities. Meanwhile, they attribute their failures to a lack of effort or a need to acquire new skills. And those with a negative frame of mind (our High-FFs) attribute their successes to the fact the task was easy or that they were lucky, and their failures to their innate lack of ability.

Weiner talked of a "locus of control" – a concept first developed by Julian B. Rotter in the 1950s – to explain the extent to which individuals believe they can shape events that have an impact upon them. Having a positive frame of mind, it seems, is based on an "internal locus of control", which results in a self-belief we can adapt or control external factors – or at least their impact upon us. A negative frame of mind is based on an "external locus of control", which results in a self-belief that we are at the whim of external forces – such as luck or fate or the manipulation of others – that we have no power to influence, and that our skills (or more likely our lack of them) are innate, which means our ability to learn new skills is limited.

Not only does this suggest a major link between negative self-beliefs and a fear of failure, it brings us right back to the High-FF's impaired evaluation abilities. High-AMs ignore the noise around them in favour of their own inner confidence and reasoning – even when evaluating their failures, which they assume are surmountable with new learning and deeper concentration. Meanwhile, High-FFs assume failures or setbacks are insurmountable because their (presumably low) skill levels are fixed.

And their poor self-beliefs mean that they are subject to any influence or signal – good or more likely bad – from outside.

Friends, family, colleagues, teachers, rivals, strangers, gurus, even celebrities and fictional characters – all offer seemingly more credible information about their detailed and particular circumstances and abilities than they can evaluate for themselves, hence making them vulnerable to the big promises of the "you can do it" self-help literature (as well as a reliance on concepts such as luck, fate or astrology).

So poor self-beliefs lead to poor evaluations (based on our fears), which lead to poor responses (also based on our fears): a horrible self-fulfilling vortex of failure. Sounds like you? It certainly sounded like me. Damn that inner doubt that made every positive move seem unsustainable (just temporary luck), while every negative happening confirmation of my own inner awfulness. Damn that poor self-belief that was willing to listen to any advice no matter how inappropriate – from no matter what source – while undermining my already fragile inner resolve. And damn that fear of failure that destroyed my academic potential as a child and my career choices as an adult in favour of the easy options or ridiculous dreams.

What's Stopping You? *You may avoid challenging but achievable tasks due to a fear of public humiliation while having no problem attempting near-impossible tasks because failure will be kindly judged (and they may mask your avoidance of achievable tasks). Unfortunately for those with fear of failure, your career and life choices can follow the same dynamic.*

2

NEURAL HIJACKINGS AND EXTERNAL RESPONSES

In his landmark book *Emotional Intelligence* (1994), Daniel Goleman describes the instant impact various emotional incidents have on the body. For instance, anger makes blood rush to the hands ready for action, while the heart rate increases and there is a surge of adrenalin. With fear, blood rushes to the skeletal muscles such as the legs, the face blanches and the body momentarily freezes as it decides whether hiding may be a better option than running or fighting. Meanwhile, there is a flood of hormones that puts the body on general alert, making us edgy and incapable of concentrating on anything other than the threat to hand.

Such a response offers obvious short-term advantages – especially if we are truly threatened. However, as Goleman says, someone experiencing these physical responses to an emotional state for any length of time is like a "car stuck in a perpetual high gear", with all the attendant physical damage this implies.

Yet it's the brain's response that causes the more permanent damage. These high-drama moments cause the amygdale – which Goleman describes as a key cluster of components in the limbic system dealing with emotions such as anxiety, distress and fear – to signal other brain regions to strengthen their memory of the incident. This creates a bigger imprint within the memory, which generates a new neural "setpoint" that can cause a lifelong resetting of the brain's default (i.e. instant) responses to even tangentially similar situations – making us respond with fear, perhaps without even realizing why.

"Such traumatic memories seem to remain as fixtures in brain function because they interfere with subsequent learning – specifically, with relearning a more normal response to those traumatising events," says Goleman.

This is not dissimilar to cases of post-traumatic stress disorder (PTSD). Like Miller's rats, both the memory and the ability to learn have gone awry – a process psychologists call "fear conditioning" in which something that is not threatening is treated as a threat simply because it's immediately associated with the past traumatic event that created the fearful default setting in the brain.

Equally importantly, the fear response arrives via a "neural hijacking" – an emotional explosion in which the limbic system proclaims an emergency, "recruiting the rest of the brain to its urgent agenda", says Goleman. This hijacking, which is instantaneous and arrives in an emotional surge, overrides what Goleman calls the "thinking brain" – leading to instant emotional responses based on fear, whatever the reality.

Post-traumatic stress disorder

I have no doubt that this is exactly what happens to those with a high fear of failure. Past traumas have hardwired fear into us, generating our own version of PTSD that leads to fear conditioning and fear responses when the memory is triggered. Yale University's Dennis Charney states in his paper *The Science of Emotion – Understanding PTSD* that studies have shown that such traumas can occur at a very early age or even in the womb (perhaps passed through the mother), so we may not even be conscious of the events that trigger our own version of PTSD.

And, crucially for High-FFs, trauma in this instance can mean incidents of public humiliation or episodes involving demeaning parents, siblings, teachers or peers. These traumas, although mild in comparison to serious cases of PTSD, can still generate fear conditioning that induces a neural hijacking when prompted. According to studies into PTSD, even brief or mild exposure to traumatic stress – especially when young – can permanently damage the hippocampus (a key part of the brain for the formation of memories), stopping normal new cell growth. This means that we will *always* evaluate information via this fearful default setting, making those neural hijackings – and the associated fear response – inevitable.

And our hormones only add to the problems. Threatening situations or other fear-inducing traumas cause the hormone cortisol to be secreted, the production of which is enormously influenced by our early upbringing.

"In normal people [cortisol] levels go up and down according to what is happening at any given moment," says Oliver James in his influential 2002 book on family survival, *They F*** You Up*, "but if we were living in a highly stressful family in our first six or so years of life [or suffered other stress] this acts like a thermostat, setting our cortisol levels too high or too low in adulthood."

James states that adults who suffered childhood traumas experience damage to their cortisol regulatory system, resulting in it either closing down, which can lead to low empathy and callousness, or becoming jammed on permanent alert, which can lead to stress, anger, anxiety and depression.

So can we be rewired to suppress Goleman's neural hijackings or normalize James's cortisol thermostat? Fears can subside over time through natural and spontaneous relearning, says Goleman (citing Charney). For instance, a child once frightened by a dog can lose their fear of that breed through strong positive contact with a similar dog later in life. Yet in many cases the distrust never entirely disappears. PTSD can prevent spontaneous relearning from *ever* occurring.

So profound can be the impact of the trauma that those neural hijackings create a fear response whenever the memory is triggered.

In fact, each reminder can add to the trauma – turning childhood fears based on traumatic early-life events into major and paralysing adult phobias. In most cases, the brain never naturally relearns a milder reaction, which means that the learning process is impaired and the fear response can only ever be diverted through intense concentration and active relearning over many years.

Daniel Goleman and high EQ

Certainly, from reading Goleman and James and other writers describing early-life trauma and its impact on the emotions I became convinced that – perhaps due to traumatic early-childhood events – High-FFs have impaired emotional responses that are not experienced by those with high achievement motivation. These responses, moreover, lead to false evaluations, which, in turn, lead to fear-based external responses – themselves leading to negative self-fulfilling results.

Those with high achievement motivation, meanwhile, are free of such negative and self-fulfilling responses. In fact High-AMs clearly have what Goleman calls high EQ (i.e. a high "emotional quotient" – comparing it to "intelligence quotient" or IQ). And such emotional competence, according to Goleman, dominates our potential for success in life (he infers by as much as 80 percent) – creating a major chasm between the achievement potential of those with high-EQ and those with low-EQ.

He lists high-EQ "competencies" as including the ability to self start, to grasp personality-based politics and to get along with people. Other positive innate high-EQ traits, meanwhile, include a concern for others, self knowledge, an ability to manage emotions, social adroitness, enthusiasm and commitment.

Of course, this also reads like a list of everything the High-FF is not. I failed on most of these counts and even those I didn't – such as enthusiasm – could easily be judged as no more than a mask to hide deeply-held insecurities.

High-FFs are capable of emotional intelligence

Emotional intelligence (or high-EQ) is therefore vital if we want to make the move towards achievement motivation. High-FFs need to develop their skills in all the above areas, which seems daunting although is far from impossible. We may be High-FFs, with all the resulting baggage, but we *are* capable of emotional intelligence, however innate our fears and insecurities. We simply need to learn it. Broken down into constituent parts, each of Goleman's traits is an attainable goal for the High-FF:

- *Ability to self start* – self-starting is little more than having direction (see Part Two), knowing how to take that first step (see Part Three) and how to keep going despite the setbacks. High-FFs need help in this respect, but help is at hand.
- *To grasp personality-based politics* – good people judgement comes from being aware of your own emotions and your own and others' objectives (see Part Four). It also comes from being strongly goal-oriented and with the emotional maturity to seek win:win outcomes. Certainly, if we are meeting our own objectives, we can help others meet theirs, and the politics subsides (although, as we shall see, sustainable progress may mean reversing the order in which this is achieved).
- *To get along with people* – many High-FFs have poor people skills, but remove the classic frustrations suffered by those with a high fear of failure and our evaluations of others should improve, making our dealings with people a lot easier (see Part Four).
- *To be concerned for others* – ditto. High-AMs can afford to be more charitable, we feel, but so can we once we have developed strong principle-centred goals and are making good progress.
- *Self knowledge* – we are rapidly acquiring this, thanks.
- *Ability to manage emotions* – aware that those neural hijackings are based on flawed evaluations and incorrect assumptions,

we can learn to create better second responses based on more positive evaluations – hopefully closer in time to the actual neural-hijacking moments. That monkey won't disappear, but we can negate the potential damage he causes.

- *Social adroitness* – another innate gift for the High-AM that we can learn. There is no social skill beyond the High-FF once we have self-awareness, are goal-oriented and have learnt some tactics and habits for motivation, task-processing and people management.
- *Enthusiasm and commitment* – no longer a mask if we are travelling the right path and making good progress towards the right goals.

Getting on top of our external responses

Our number one concern at this stage, however, is to get on top of our external responses to those neural hijackings – in other words to attack the symptoms of our fear of failure. Whether this is anger, frustration, anxiety or depression, these are the external responses that generate many of the poor self-fulfilling results for the High-FF.

So if we can understand what we are feeling, and why, we may be able to start the process of creating better second responses and therefore begin to undermine those self-fulfilling behavioural changes. This is unlikely to be easy, and nothing below is written flippantly, yet self-awareness can help trigger the process of turning our thinking in a more positive direction, which will hopefully – in time and with many small self-confirming steps – change those external responses, or at least reduce their impact.

Perhaps the easiest external response to understand is the most extreme: anger. Anger is fear's ugly sister, so while fear remains the hidden Cinderella, its noisy sibling is out and proud and extremely menacing. As emotions go, anger is by far the most apparent, as well as the most destructive because, not only do we lose control over our feelings, we lose control over our actions – sometimes destroying strong, long-term, constructive activity in seconds.

"No other emotion – anxiety, depression, even love – erases our control so completely," write health practitioner Carl Semmelroth and psychologist Donald E.P. Smith in *The Anger Habit* (2000).

And anger goes way beyond pure rage. As Semmelroth and Smith note, critical thoughts, revenge fantasies and paranoid interpretations of others' behaviour can all provide the context for anger, whether we outwardly boil over, show irritation or inwardly seethe.

Anger as concealment and control

One route to overcoming anger is to understand its purpose. Anger is often an act of concealment, a way of hiding our inner feelings of guilt or confusion or hurt or – most likely – fear.

As US family counsellor Carol D. Jones writes in her 2004 book *Overcoming Anger*: "It's just plain easier to tell yourself you're mad [i.e. angry] than it is to say you're sad, confused, hurt or frightened."

That's a powerful admission and one likely to chime with many High-FFs: it's not anger, stupid, it's fear.

And the fact anger is mostly an external manifestation is a clue to its other core purpose. According to *The Anger Habit* anger is often an attempt to control others. The angry person perceives they are in a contest for power, and they are losing (hence the fear). Things are not falling into place as they had hoped, so they are trying to change the situation through coercion.

"Anger tells us that we are preparing to force others, or ourselves, to comply with some expectation," it concludes.

Both *The Anger Habit* and *Overcoming Anger* focus on awareness and acceptance as the key ingredients for overcoming anger. Angry people must accept that the root cause of their anger is not the other person's behaviour but their own core beliefs and their inner feelings of fear and inadequacy.

Meanwhile, the godfather of motivational gurus, Anthony Robbins, goes a little easier on anger. In *Awaken the Giant Within* (1992) he sees anger, like other emotions, as an "action signal". Anger can be a positive, he claims, if we "turn that emotional intensity into directed excitement and passion". Many angry people feel locked in a cycle of fear and frustration, with their anger demonstrating their clear desire to unlock the cage and get going in a more rewarding direction. The motivation is there, but rattling the cage won't get us on our way. We need to find a key. And that takes planning (see Part Two).

Frustration and anxiety

Of course this brings us neatly to frustration, anger's little brother. Anthony Robbins also has a lot to say about frustration. He sees it as an exciting action signal because frustration actually comes from a sense of inner self-belief that we could and should be in a better place. It says the solution is within range but that we need to change our approach. In this respect, frustration is very different to disappointment, which is a more final feeling – of negative acceptance – that we are defeated and will never attain what we seek.

Anxiety, meanwhile, is less easily dismissed and is, in fact, a symptom of PTSD – a long-term reaction to the continual triggering of the fear response. As we have seen, such triggering leads to avoidance of situations in which we may be triggered, with anxiety the response to even the prospect of such situations. Yet, according to Glen R. Schiraldi in *The Post-Traumatic Stress Disorder Sourcebook* (2000), anxious people can become conditioned to fear even the tactics or distractions they use to avoid the fear response.

For instance, the earlier child frightened by the dog may become anxious at even the prospect of contacting a similar dog – maybe in a park or along a footpath – perhaps changing her route to school because of it, with even the new route eventually triggering anxiety because of its association with the original trauma. And it takes no great leaps to apply such anxiety-based behaviour to the avoidance tactics of Atkinson's High-FF children.

Reversing this self-fulfilling cycle of fear and worry is no mean feat, and usually involves professional help. But, as Schiraldi states, we can learn to confront our anxieties through the acceptance of our condition and, through therapy, the erection of protective "boundaries" as well as the avoidance of "retraumatizing behaviours" (such as alcohol).

And we can also take tiny steps towards a less anxious future, perhaps learning over time to reframe our concerns by focusing on the positive, by not trying to right past wrongs (revenge fantasies stoke up rather than reduce anxiety) and by forcing objective evaluations onto any anxiety-inducing situation (hopefully closer in time to the situation itself) – all as recommended by Dale Carnegie, one of the most famous self-improvement writers of the 20th century in *How to Stop Worrying and Start Living* (1948).

Depression is a thief

Which brings us to depression, "Depression is a thief that steals from people, robbing them of energy, vitality, self-esteem and any pleasure that they might previously have enjoyed," writes Irish psychologist Tony Bates in *Understanding and Overcoming Depression* (2001).

Depression is typified by an unrelenting sad mood, an absence of energy, a problem in concentrating or remembering, a loss of interest in activities once enjoyed and difficulties with sleeping and eating. In many ways it is the flipside to anger – an emotional response based on feelings of defeat and withdrawal, making anger seem like a positive fighting response in comparison.

Yet Bates's recommendations for treating depression strike a chord with our programme for aiding those with fear of failure. Awareness of the root causes – such as negative early-life experiences or harsh, demeaning or controlling parents or other sown seeds for low self-esteem – is a major step, as well as knowledge of the destructive thought patterns that spiral into depression. We can attack these with deliberate attempts to more positively reframe our thoughts, he states, and by taking small actionable steps that slowly lift the clouds.

"Recovery from depression is a journey rather than a destination," says Bates, echoing the sentiments of this book on both fear of failure and low self-esteem.

Yet Robbins is more forthright on depression – holding the depressed person responsible for his or her condition.

"In order to be depressed," he says in his seminal work *Unlimited Power* (1987), "you have to view your life in specific ways."

It takes effort to do this, he states, involving what we say to ourselves and in what tone. It also involves how we hold ourselves and how we breathe. And it involves playing games with our blood-sugar levels through poor diet and excessive alcohol.

"Some people have created this state so often though, that it is easy to produce," says Robbins – pointing out that to many it can actually feel like the most comforting state to be in, helped by secondary gains such as sympathy from others and allowances from peers. But we had to work at getting ourselves into such a bad place, he says, just as we can and should work to get ourselves out of it.

Taking responsibility

Far from being callous, Robbins's tough-love approach hits upon an important concept for any High-FF hoping to develop achievement motivation. We need to take responsibility for our thoughts and actions, as well as our emotional and external responses, no matter how they manifest themselves. This is a theme that runs right through the motivational universe and is something we *must* grasp, not least because any form of progress is impossible if we continue to blame others (parents, siblings, peers, teachers) for who we are and how we respond.

Whatever your personal history, no one else is responsible for *your* actions and *your* behaviour, or even *your* inner thoughts, evaluations and responses. *You* are. Blame is simply an excuse for inaction. Meanwhile, taking responsibility is the quickest route for turning those feelings of fear, frustration, anger or depression into better responses.

In *The Seven Habits of Highly Effective People* (1989), Stephen Covey makes it clear that anyone seeking self improvement needs to take complete responsibility for their responses in every situation. In probably the most important statement in what is *the* most influential self-help book in this area, Covey writes "it isn't what happens to us that counts, it's how we respond".

He actually wrote: "between stimulus and response man has the freedom to choose", but it is such a vital concept, I thought it important to put it in language that would help us remember it (Covey also wrote "in choosing our response to circumstances, we powerfully affect our circumstances," which is equally memorable).

In other words, we may not be responsible for the external forces that intrude upon our lives – or, indeed, for what generated our self-beliefs in early childhood – but as adults, we are 100 percent responsible for our evaluation of such forces, as well as the impact we allow them to have upon us and, most importantly, our responses.

The answer is not to deny responsibility (or "response-ability" as Covey prefers to construct it) by blaming others and circumstances. The answer is to embrace it. Taking responsibility for our past failures and current predicaments – and even our feelings – is a fantastically liberating concept. Just imagine if you were totally responsible for where you are today, even in terms of how you feel inwardly. Awful as that may seem – discomforting as it is – it is also wonderfully empowering. It means you are totally responsible for your future. It is in *your* hands.

Focus on the present and future

Taking responsibility is a giant leap towards achievement motivation – regaining Weiner's "locus of control" even if the current self-view is a negative one. (Covey also stresses that we may have to accept a negatively-assessed starting point.) Another is to recognize something equally important – that everything up until the moment we read this sentence is in the past. And that we *cannot change the past.*

"Put the past in the past and focus on the present," said Dale Carnegie (1948). In fact he wrote "shut out the yesterdays which have lighted fools the way to dusty death," but such prose can be off-putting to modern readers.

Carnegie blamed the past – and obsessing about past mistakes – as one of the central causes of worry in people. It is also a core reason why that monkey always has the last word – citing past failures as evidence that the future will be no different.

Yet the monkey is lying because he couldn't possibly know. Just as the past cannot be changed, the future cannot be known. So we can choose to approach the future with fear – by listening to the monkey – or we can decide that the past is only relevant as a learning tool for the present and future.

And by, first, taking responsibility for our actions and emotions, and, second, accepting that we cannot change anything from the past, we have, indeed, taken control of our present, which is a pretty liberating thought.

What's Stopping You? *"Fear conditioning" triggers "neural hijackings" that generate fearful responses. Such conditioning may have developed from early-life traumas. To make progress, you must accept this and take total responsibility for your responses when triggered.*

3

FAILURE AS A POSITIVE EXPERIENCE

Can failure ever be positive? Of course, if that's how we decide to view it. View it as a milestone or lesson on the way to success, then that's what it will be. View it, instead, as a final and total condemnation of your character and – indeed – that too will be the near-certain result.

My writing "career" is a strong case in point with respect to the self-fulfilling nature of our view of failure. Having spent the last 18 months of my banking career "reverse commuting" to Greenwich, Connecticut, I used the journey to write about my experiences as a single British lad living in New York. Typed up in the evenings, I soon had around 60,000 words and was looking for a literary agent. By some miracle (in fact, good research and hard lobbying) I landed one of the most respected literary agents in the business, who landed me a publishing deal with one of the UK's largest and most respected publishers.

I had hooped the distant peg, and whooped around my Upper Westside apartment like a man whose life had changed forever. I was set for a career wandering the globe as a humorous writer. And while from this distance such a response looks a bit silly, the joke wasn't entirely on me. Both the agent and the publisher said the book sold well, although I was disappointed it hadn't sold in its hundreds of thousands. In fact, that was a key reason for my failure with respect to my book-writing career – I understood nothing of the book-publishing world so had no way to gauge my expectations.

Failure is a question of interpretation

Ultimately, I failed as a writer because that's how I decided to interpret it. By all accounts, a major house publishing my autobiographical first book while I was still in my early 30s was a strong first step as an author. Sure, it hadn't sold as many as I'd hoped but there were some lessons to learn regarding marketing such a book and making sure the publisher is fully onside with respect to distribution – and, indeed, with respect to ensuring the author has realistic expectations regarding sales.

But I dismissed this in favour of the view that it was a total failure, because it failed to "breakthrough" and turn me into an overnight Nick Hornby. With no fame on offer I opted for the monkey's interpretation that its failure to make headlines was a final confirmation of my innate awfulness. As for the lessons, what was the point of them? They'd never be implemented because I'd blown my *only* chance to make it.

And such feelings changed my behaviour – rendering me incapable of rationality when dealing, first, with the publisher and then with the agent – not helped by an inevitable dose of writer's block for a second book (inevitable because the confidence with which I'd written the original book had evaporated). Before long I'd been thrown out of the author's club altogether.

Of course, I realize now that my behaviour had been that of a classic High-FF. Someone with high achievement motivation would have taken time to consolidate the achievement by controlling the marketing, cultivating the right people and deeply researching the next topic. This was no more than a debut book, the content of which should reflect my values for a future writing career (not the publisher's – who may have a very different idea of the book's potential audience). And if it failed to make the bestseller's list? Well, it was a lot to ask for a first book and there are lessons to get me further up the ladder next time.

High-FFs, however, react with amazement at the prospect of success and immediately develop inappropriate and undermining behaviour while, in reality, losing control of the project and therefore the direction it will take them. And, of course, the second the results fail to match our probably-unrealistic expectations we collapse – condemning ourselves as a fool for having ever thought we could aim so high. We are crap people, we conclude, forever condemned to our lowly status – not realising that we have chosen this response from the range of conclusions on offer, some of which were far from condemning.

The link with low self-esteem

While the above interpretation of failure is, as stated, the classic view of the High-FF, it also reveals another personality trait that cannot be ignored when dealing with fear of failure: low self-esteem. Of course, fear of failure and low self-esteem are different afflictions: fear of failure undermines our actions (changing our behaviour), while low self-esteem distorts our beliefs (generating negative evaluations). But, like fear of failure, low self-esteem is a self-fulfilling condition – leading us to evaluate the world in ways that encourage their external confirmation (that we will fail, or that we are worthless).

And while not all High-FFs have low self-esteem (or vice versa), fear of failure and low self-esteem are inextricably and obviously linked. They are fellow travellers – afflictions that feed off each other as much as they feed off their host – meaning that any programme for progress for High-FFs that ignores low self-esteem leaves a gaping and unbridgeable hole in the road.

As with fear, feelings of low self-esteem stem from our experiences from a very young age but are reinforced by what we are told and what we experience, and how we interpret such information, as we become adults. Such feedback – as well as the unconditional love and acceptance (or otherwise) from parents, teachers, siblings and peers – forms our inner beliefs, perceptions, conclusions and predictions for life.

Of course, such self-beliefs can be a distortion. According to John Caunt in his very practical 2003 book *Boost Your Self Esteem*, no one is an unbiased observer of themselves. Misrepresentations, omissions and exaggerations can all distort our self-beliefs, resulting in low self-esteem, when the same information presented differently could have generated entirely different conclusions. In fact, many highly-successful people suffer from low self-esteem, dismissing their achievements as worthless while ignoring the fact observers may be in awe of those very accomplishments.

"There is no automatic link between one's competence and the level of one's self esteem," writes Caunt.

Our lives are shaped not by events, says Caunt, but by our responses to those events (echoing Covey), "and the way we respond will be largely dictated by our self-beliefs".

But we *can* change our beliefs, believes Caunt. We have developed one set of beliefs and have given them importance, so we can do the same thing again. We can create our own reality. We can even manipulate our thoughts, says Caunt. So far in our life we have manipulated them negatively to generate low self-esteem – so why not manipulate them for a more positive purpose?

Reframing failure

Yet this is easier said than done, in my view. Hardwired or default settings mean that any newly-imposed thoughts or beliefs will feel like they are going against the grain, which will result in setbacks or failures being judged as confirmations that the original settings were the correct ones. That monkey won't shift so easily, I'm afraid.

But I may be taking Caunt too literally. What if we tried to reframe negative influences, not to change our inner beliefs or default settings but in order to soften or even alter their impact? We will look at reframing the negative assumptions that underline low self-esteem in Part Four but what about failure? Can we reframe our view of failure – perhaps even rethinking failure as something to embrace as a necessary part of the journey? Would that change the way we view failure – maybe even helping to reduce our fear of it? Maybe even helping me see the collapse of my writing career in a better light?

Maybe. As we have seen, those paralysed by fear of failure go to great lengths to avoid public humiliation, including avoiding tasks or careers that may mean contact with the consequences of failure. But, as Alain de Botton says in *Status Anxiety*, fear of failure would not be so great if failure were not so harshly viewed. The world is unsympathetic to failure, referring to those that fail as "losers" – a word, according to de Botton, "callously signifying both that people have lost and that they have at the same time forfeited any right to sympathy for having done so".

Depersonalizing failure

This is tough, but is it true? At a primary level, yes of course. We all have to secretly hide our inner joy even at a friend's misfortunes. And with our enemies and rivals we don't bother to hide it. How many dinner parties have been dominated by the delighted chatter of negative gossip about a mutual acquaintance?

Such *schadenfreude* is classic competitive behaviour that any primatologist (those that study primates) would understand. Yet while this may suggest we have the wrong friends, it is more likely to suggest that we are looking at failure too personally. Exchange personal failure for company or organizational failure and attitudes change considerably. This is because companies are not people. They are a collection of people and machines brought together for an – often highly-specialized – common goal.

In other words, they are a project. And the failure of a project may dent the reputation and even the self-esteem of those involved. But it is by no means a final and fatal condemnation of the people – just of the project itself. The people involved simply start again, a little bruised, a little wiser, but certainly not forever condemned.

And if we could look at individual failure this way perhaps the crushing enormity and finality of it can be reduced. While not eliminating the pain, surely we can reduce the extent to which a single or series of setbacks confirms our poor self beliefs? Most High-FFs view any failure as absolute, as a confirmation of their personal and irreversible lack of aptitude. But if we could see it as a project, as just one result, we may be able to look beyond the pain, or at least not be derailed by it.

For instance, the loss of my writing career was only a "loss" because I chose to treat it as such. High-AMs would have seen publication as a strong first step, with further thought required for that "difficult second book" – not its "failure" as an irretrievable condemnation of my abilities as a book writer. Indeed, they would have learnt the lessons – realizing that the project was clearly flawed but book writing as a career choice was far from dead (I'd won over two of the most respected literary institutions in London, after all). It was my negative self beliefs that made it final.

Despite what High-FFs think, failure is never absolute. According to Anthony Robbins, as long as a person breathes and is willing to act, there is nothing final about failure. So why should it be so personal? Is it not just one result, brought about by a range of circumstances some of which were beyond our control?

Seeing failure this way is a difficult task for High-FFs because it tells us to develop the mind of the High-AM, who is willing to learn from negative experiences and make small adjustments in the knowledge that goal attainment is not only possible but probable – even inevitable. They don't need to depersonalize failure because they will not view it personally in the first place. Why should they, when they know success is within their grasp?

But High-FFs need tools to get to this point, of which developing a mental depersonalization of their progress, or otherwise, could be one. If we could think of ourselves as companies – as *Me Inc.*

or *Me Ltd.* rather than just *me* – and our progress as a project, then we should be able to put failure in its place: as a mere setback rather than the ultimate condemnation of our self worth.

Company failure is a transformed concept

And failure from the perspective of a company is a transformed concept. Tom Peters is perhaps the best known company guru of all. In his well-known book *In Search of Excellence* (written with Robert H. Waterman Jr. in 1982) he quotes senior industry figures such as the heads of Johnson & Johnson and engineering giant Emerson extolling not just the benefits of failure but its absolute requirement as an experience for leadership.

In fact, finding successful company executives promoting the virtues of failure is easy. They all seem to love talking about it:

"Success is not built on success. It's built on failure. It's built on frustration. Sometimes it's built on catastrophe" – Sumner Redstone, majority owner of MTV, CBS, Dreamworks, Paramount Pictures, and others.

"Surviving a failure gives you more self-confidence. Failures are great learning tools" – Jeremy Immelt, Chairman and CEO of General Electric.

There are hundreds of such quotes.

Some of the most innovative companies even build failure into their business model. According to Tom Peters, *3M* (inventors of the Post-it Note and much else besides) guarantees product managers the ability to run with their inventions backed up by a commitment to total job security should they fail.

In his seminar-turned-book *Crazy Times Call for Crazy Organizations* (1994), Tom Peters furthers his theme by railing at those bosses that cringe at the thought of failure while celebrating those that embrace it.

On Richard Branson he quotes his publisher John Brown: "The whole secret of Branson's success is his failures . . . He keeps opening things and a good many of them fail – but he doesn't give a f*** – he keeps on going."

Failing is not the problem, according to Tom Peters – far from it. Failure is absolutely necessary. It is fear of failure that is the principal cause of paralysis in companies, whether it is the receptionist or the CEO. To overcome this he recommends that companies adopt a culture of failure. Of course, this is fine for small failures but that is not enough for Peters. Every now and again the failure has to be "big, bold, embarrassing, face-losing and public". Companies that do not make utter fools of themselves from time to time have become smug, according to Peters, and have therefore stopped growing.

"Fail better"

And while this is a more difficult thing for individuals to accept, it should at least allow us to keep going after experiencing a setback – allowing us to focus on learning the lesson while retaining our focus on the ultimate goal. The most commonly-used quote at this point involves Thomas Edison's attempts to invent something (it ranges from the light bulb to synthetic rubber).

"I have not failed," he says after so many unsuccessful attempts at his invention. "I've just found 10,000 ways that won't work."

This chimes with Anthony Robbins in *Unlimited Power*. He states that there are no failures in life – there are only results. If the result was not what we wanted, we should learn from the experience and make better decisions in the future. Indeed, this adds an important caveat to Tom Peters. It says that failure for its own sake – while refreshing – is pointless. The point is to learn from failure. To plunge in, make mistakes, recognize the mistake, learn and try again.

To offer another over-used quote – this time from Samuel Beckett in *Worstward Ho* (1983): "Ever tried. Ever failed. No matter. Try again. Fail again. Fail better."

The key is not to seek failure but to not fear it: to embrace failure, even personal failure, as part of the journey.

This is an important realization for the High-FF. Not only are setbacks in many cases self-fulfilling due to our fear of failure and the corresponding changes in behaviour this brings, when setbacks do occur – as they will – we must condition ourselves to accept that they are by no means final. They are a result, but not *the* result. In fact, they are still probably a good result as we can learn the lesson, regroup, and do it again with greater wisdom ("fail better" indeed).

Such setbacks only condemn us as bad people – as being innately awful – if that's how we decide to interpret them. They are only final if we blow the whistle for full-time ourselves. But it's our whistle. We can blow it when we like.

What's Stopping You? *You may have a tendency to interpret temporary setbacks as a final condemnation. Yet failure is only final if you judge it so. Most failures are in fact positive learning experiences that can lead to strong progress. Depersonalization is an important tool for helping you to realize this.*

4

PRODUCING BETTER RESPONSES

The UK's NHS is a big beast of a health service, although I doubt its founders considered it would one day be a major resource for attacking low self-esteem in the good citizens of Great Britain and Northern Ireland. Yet, extraordinarily, that's where I found myself not long after my humiliating and drawn-out failure as a writer: in counselling sessions in, of all places, a London sexual health clinic.

In their wisdom, some of the more innovative NHS Trusts had realized that many sexual health problems arise from behaviours stemming from self-esteem issues, especially amongst the young. They reasoned that, while those with high self-esteem are having stable relationships with clear long-term goals in mind (even if there is a periodic change of long-term partner), those with low self-esteem pursue low-grade sexual gratification with as many partners as possible, which – as often as not – ultimately involves a trip to the clinic.

And while my own route to the sessions was more tangential, there I sat in one-to-one sessions discussing my poor childhood relationship with my father, as well as the trauma of my family splitting in two when I was a 10-year-old boy. This event, I realized from my chats with the female counsellor, left me with a life-long fear of rejection from both senior figures (representing my father) and peers (representing my sister, who had also high-tailed it with dad).

Cognitive behavioural therapy

The sessions soon ran their course and my benign cuddle from the NHS had to give way to something more constructive. I was offered a programme on cognitive behavioural therapy (CBT), which seemed to be where the counsellor was heading from early on. As the name suggests, CBT is a behavioural methodology for linking our thoughts, our feelings and our actions to try and generate more positive outcomes. For people with anxiety, depression, panic, phobias, stress and PTSD many NHS Trusts have become keen on prescribing some form of CBT.

CBT works through breaking down problems into thoughts, emotions, physical feelings and actions, and by trying to turn unhelpful perceptions of each into more helpful ones. The literature I was given used an example of being blanked by an acquaintance in the street. The unhelpful route went something like this: thoughts (I was ignored so am not liked); emotions (rejection, sadness, loss of confidence); physical feelings (low energy, depression, sickness); actions (avoidance, isolation).

Meanwhile, the helpful version went something like this: thoughts (he/she seemed distracted so something must be wrong); emotions (concern); physical feelings (none); actions (contact the person to check they are OK).

As you can probably guess, I didn't attend the course. Why? I reasoned that it was time I could better use, it was all a bit touchy-feely, and that – going by the example above – I'd be spending my time with assorted under-employed undesirables. I'd enjoyed my sessions with the counsellor but surely things had not got so bad that I had to fall back on state-sponsored group therapy?

Of course, the above feelings and thoughts are outrageously inappropriate and are almost certainly part of a High-FF response to something that was clearly going to be challenging. I feared failure at CBT and therefore avoided it – inventing an excuse that would protect my self-esteem. If I'd genuinely felt the above

I could have found sessions full of angst-ridden professionals or even seen if the counsellor was prepared to help me offline from the NHS.

Start a diary

The CBT literature, however, contained one nugget that was to transform my perceptions and evaluations overnight. It was a bullet point tucked away on an inside page under the heading: *CBT – the work*. It stated that "the therapist may ask you to keep a diary, to help identify patterns and thoughts, emotions, physical feelings and actions".

This was a coincidence as – fed up with being in a bad or depressed mood – I'd wondered whether my moods were altered by my diet and had started jotting down notes in a page-per-week diary sent by a supplier. I'd started testing my moods against the time of day, days of the week, seasons and even the phases of the moon (easy in the better diaries). And, before long, I was no longer just writing "mood" but adding descriptions such as "self-loathing" or "irritation".

Yet the CBT documents were suggesting a whole new level of journal-keeping – recording what I was feeling, as well as why I felt this way and how I was responding. I bought an A5 page-per-day diary and started writing it all down. I quickly became addicted. I found that recording my moods helped to rationalize them. My neural hijackings – while still frequent and unwelcome – seemed to dissipate almost as soon as I starting writing about them, although the pen indentations on the page still attest to the state I was some-times in.

And I also noticed from my furtive loiterings in the self-help sections of bookshops that just about every self-help book told me to keep a diary, or "journal" to use the more American word. Some were stricter than others in what they required recording but many seemed to include versions of the following.

Moods: any episodes of anger, depression, frustration, hurt. The aim is to be as explicit as possible and to record your feelings at the time. So if you felt something like: "that Johnson's done it again – he's stolen my idea the totally brainless idiot who couldn't have a single unique thought of his own but will probably end up my boss *arrrgghhhhhh*" then that's what you write down.

Having said this, it may also help to leave a space under it for a more reflective comment. This could range from "it turns out Johnson told the boss it was my idea. He is a good guy, so why was my first reaction so angry?" to "I need to get Johnson onside. My feelings towards him are irrational and undermining me – my move" to "I'm still angry about this but thank God the anger only appeared here and wasn't shouted across the entire fifth floor".

Obstacles: "No matter how prepared you are," says Anthony Robbins, "you are going to hit a few rocks along the river of life." The diary is the place to record these rocks and try and formulate a way around them. Just writing problems down can create a clarity-of-thought that removes the emotional clutter.

Goals: we'll come to the big stuff in Part Two but the day-to-day diary is for the small stuff. What's the next step? What's the time-frame? Who do I call to work out what the next step is? In fact, this is the most important aspect of the diary – making your diary the key tool for recording those small, positive, victory-by-victory building blocks of achievement. As stated, High-FFs need to create a map to chart their progress. Your diary *is* that map.

Results: how did the next step go? Did the call get the result you wanted? Yes, how come? What's next? No, why? What went wrong? Again, what's next?

Controlling displacement activity: I used to record my alcohol units. Then I realized I was drinking too much and used the diary to record progress towards keeping my intake to my weekly limit. When this kept failing I gave up drinking and now put a zero in that corner every day. Too much time on the Internet or watching TV is also recorded – again with an admonishment.

Self-flagellation: anyone reading my diary (heaven forbid – this is the most private of documents) would be shocked at how hard I am on myself. Yet that's the point. High-FFs beat themselves up all the time. I'm not asking you to stop beating yourself up – just that you do it constructively. Any beatings need to involve a "lessons learnt" element as well as practical next steps.

Self-congratulation: but also record the triumphs. I use a tick system to note what I am pleased with. The creation of new, more positive, neural pathways in the brain involves tiny steps taken in the right direction. Over time, this will build your confidence and move you towards a better place. It's an exciting journey but it *must* be recorded if the steps taken are to lead anywhere sustainable.

Experiences: I love rereading my diary from my wedding day, or when my first son was born, or the crazy day my second son was born and my first son ended up in hospital. It has helped me record the ups and downs of my life and cured me from that horrible High-FF habit of looking back and only seeing the bad stuff. I can honestly say that the years since starting my diary have been the best of my life – and I think writing a diary helped me not only remember that but realize it.

And if you think writing a diary embarrassing or cheesy or a bit angst ridden and prepubescent: fine. Get over it and write the diary anyway. If you stop reading this book now – never mind – but please start writing a diary. It is the single most transformative action you may ever take.

What's Stopping You? *A major step towards negating the poor responses caused by neural hijackings is to use a diary to record and evaluate your thoughts. It will also be your map for plotting and recording your progress.*

PART TWO
Goals

5

ACT

In Part One I wrote that the most important line in Stephen Covey's *Seven Habits of Highly Effective People* involves our responses to external events, and the fact those responses are more important than the event itself. Well, another line runs it a close second: "Act or be acted upon."

He goes on to say that "the difference between people who exercise initiative and those who don't is literally the difference between night and day".

This is another of those universal recommendations across the self-help cosmos. Without proactivity we are lost, they all seem to agree. And, as with taking responsibility, this is at once a depressing but also liberating statement. A key factor in making progress involves our own actions – not those of somebody who may or may not like us, or may or may not take pity on us, or may or may not have our best interests at heart.

We no longer have to wait for that knight in shining armour. We *are* that knight in shining armour. To be able to act ourselves means that we are no longer acted upon. We are no longer someone else's tool, enslaved to their actions. It is *our* actions that matter, not those of a higher being or "saviour", or parent, teacher, boss or friend. And once we act we are expressing ourselves as an adult, potentially for the first time.

To be proactive is therefore a giant leap towards high achievement motivation. Yet Covey warns us that proactive thinking is very different from positive thinking. By being proactive we are assessing things as they stand, which may be at their most negative. There is no gloss. It is what it is. Nonetheless, we are also stating that we are able, and that we are willing, to do something about it.

Circle of influence

But do something about what? In order to be effective we need boundaries for our proactivity. And, luckily, Covey offers them – via a major point of mental differentiation. Any transformation to a more productive place requires the correct focus for our energies, which Covey maps by describing all external inputs into our life as being part of our Circle of Concern. However, some of these inputs are completely beyond our control, such as the weather, the traffic, or the actions of governments or large corporations.

What we can influence within the Circle of Concern – such as our own wellbeing and our work and home life – he calls our Circle of Influence. Obviously, this is a smaller circle, although it is the area that should be the focus of our every action. Anybody trying to take action to make progress in their life should concern themselves only with what they *can* change – their Circle of Influence – leaving alone those areas where they have no influence either physically or mentally.

It is the world of the reactive person, Covey states, to spend their lives feeling angry and powerless (and even victimized) by what they perceive as the forces lined up against them, which – of course – they are helpless to do anything about. Proactive people, meanwhile, change what is changeable by focusing only on what is within their Circle of Influence.

Goals are a major differentiator

Having calculated that action is required and reconciled ourselves to the zone where action is possible, we now need to direct that action. Any step is only a step forward if it is a step in the right direction. And that requires a plan. Without plans with discernable objectives we are directionless, and directionless people are either stuck in the same place or condemned to going round in circles.

"Without goals you simply drift and flow on the currents of life," wrote sales motivator Brian Tracy in his best-selling book *Goals!* (2003). "With goals, you fly like an arrow straight and true to your target."

Tracy describes life without goals as being similar to driving in thick fog. No matter how powerful the car, we drive slowly and hesitantly, making little progress. Clear goals, meanwhile, enable us to "step on the accelerator".

Goals, therefore, make a big difference to both those that set them, and those that don't.

Outsourcing our ambitions

Yet for the High-FF, our fate can be worse than simply watching the goal-setters progress while we get left behind. We are often recruited to help execute *their* plans, sometimes under the false premise that their goals are also our own. This was very much my experience when starting out as an entrepreneur at Metrocube – my partner spotting my directionless post-banking pursuits and recruiting me as the executer of his own goals (with near-disastrous results for our partnership – see Part Five).

Indeed, in the absence of our own plan, we may as well adopt their goals. Those with a plan inspire confidence in others so, if we are directionless, we are bound to follow them. How can we make a decision if we don't know where we are going? How can we lead even ourselves? Decisions and leadership are for those that have direction, so directionless people often end up feeling they are best-off outsourcing their ambitions – even their decision-making – to someone who appears more able, simply because they have defined goals.

According to Steve Chandler in *100 Ways to Motivate Yourself* (2001) in "life today, you are either living your dream or living someone else's. And unless you give your own dream the time and space it needs . . . you'll simply help others make their dreams come true".

Yet many High-FFs perceive themselves to be frustrated by others – usually High-AMs who seem to block our way while the path for them appears open. The difference between them and us, however, is often no more than the fact they are pursuing a detailed and preconceived plan and we are simply being dragged along by seemingly greater but invisible forces.

The grey zone

Goals also prevent us from entering what neuro-linguistic programming practitioner (more on NLP later) Lindsey Agness calls in *Change Your Life with NLP* (2008) the "grey zone". This is where most High-FFs spend their lives: not destitute, quite comfortable even, but stuck and tremendously frustrated. It is a settlement for second best that will eat away at your happiness daily unless you enter what she calls the "awful zone" where things become so bad action becomes essential.

I can remember almost wishing for the awful zone to come – some disastrous moment that cleared the slate and allowed me to start again. I used to call it my "virtual suicide". With nothing to lose, I would surely lose my fear, I thought. Yet that day never arrived because I never made it happen. Instead I remained trapped in avoidance activities – simply "making a living" rather than in designing a rewarding and fulfilling life. Goals, of course, would have circumnavigated the need for a "virtual suicide". Goals would have allowed me to see and plot a path upwards without having to hit rock-bottom first.

This leads on to what is perhaps the most fantastic thing about goal setting: the fact that the journey itself generates such a sense of excitement that we experience something of the sensation of arrival from the moment we take that first step. This is obvious to all but those with a high fear of failure simply because we have always been terrified of that first step. Yet we experience the same feeling when travelling. Just knowing that the destination is the airport and, after that, some exotic land of adventure makes that familiar first-leg drive through our home town that much sweeter.

Brian Tracy agrees with this, writing in *Goals!* that: "Goal-setting is so powerful that the very act of *thinking* about your goals makes you happy even before you have taken the first step towards achieving them".

Given this, imagine how you will feel after just a few positive and reaffirming steps along the path.

Tracy states that strong goals will make "you feel internally motivated to get up and get going every morning because every step you are taking will be moving you in the direction of something that is important to you".

Avoiding avoidance goals

Goal setting also reverses the psyche in the most profound way possible.

Tracy again: "Successful people think about what they want and how to get it," he writes, "while unsuccessful and unhappy people think about what they don't want and talk about their problems and worries and who is to blame."

Anthony Robbins (1992) wrote that the human mind is always in pursuit of an objective (Aristotle backs this up, opining that humans are a "teleological" organism, which means we are always moving towards something). So if we are not pursuing positive goals, says Robbins, we are pursuing the goal of eliminating or avoiding pain. These are negative or avoidance goals but, for the High-FF, they are probably the only real goals we have ever set.

Robbins states that it is the unconscious fear of disappointment that stops many people from setting positive and appropriate goals. Some may previously have set positive goals and failed to achieve them – resulting in an overwhelming fear of inflicting further pain. And this has led us to abandon positive goal-setting in order to avoid any renewed expectations also being dashed.

Yet the answer is not to hide from the pursuit of goals. The answer is to set the right goals. And these take time to calculate.

Setting the right goals

So what *do* you want? As a High-FF you will need to have an acute awareness of the fact you may set inappropriate goals – at both extremes – for fear of Atkinson's High-FF peg-hooping avoidance tactics mentioned in Part One. You may yet aim too low or too high because you secretly view yourself as incapable of achieving even moderately challenging goals.

So how can you tell if you have the right goals – other than by waiting for potentially the wrong result? Not easy. For instance, at Moorgate we often discuss with clients the need to look beneath the surface when it comes to setting objectives for our PR campaigns. The client can think we spend too much time on this, sometimes stating in irritation "it's obvious isn't it – to win new business?"

But properly brainstorming objectives can reveal that the real goals are not always the obvious ones. There have been times when we have set the wrong objectives, which has led to the wrong strategy and the wrong tactics (more on strategy and tactics in Part Three) – something that has sometimes only become apparent after achieving the wrong results.

For instance, we had one banking client whose stated objective was to win new clients. Yet he was determined to do this by profiling himself in the international financial press, although his clients were very clearly specialists in local markets. He was unimpressed by trade or regional publications, he stated, and thought a profile in the *Financial Times* or *Wall Street Journal* the only way to get noticed.

Of course, we failed to win him the coverage he wanted as his messages were too audience-specific. Yet when we dug further it turned out his real objective was to impress his bosses who were thinking of cutting funding for the department. This knowledge meant we could change the strategy and tactics accordingly – eventually creating a series of newsletters that detailed his deal successes and included interviews with happy clients. We then circulated them both internally (upstairs) and externally to new or potential clients. He was delighted with the results.

This is no less the case with our own lives. Just being busy and taking action is pointless unless we are pursuing the right goals, which are not always obvious. Covey writes about getting caught up in "busy-ness" or the "activity trap". He states that if the ladder is not leaning against the right wall then every step up just takes us further from our real goals. We are heading to the wrong place faster.

So what will lead you to set the right goals? And how can you trust that your goals are the right ones? This takes some intense visualization, some deep thinking and some soul-searching – all of which is to come.

What's Stopping You? *Without proactivity you are condemned to make no progress in your life. And without goals you are prone to becoming the tools of those with goals. Yet strong goal-setting can generate excitement and positivity before you have even taken the first step.*

6

VISUALIZATION

In the previous chapter I quoted from Lindsey Agness's book *Change Your Life With NLP*. Now seems like a good moment to discuss NLP or neuro-linguistic programming given that this section – on visualization of goals – owes more than a little to that happy band of self motivators. Many modern self-help books are either openly or indirectly using NLP in their framework of actions. And millions of people with low self-esteem or low confidence have undoubtedly had their lives improved by adopting NLP techniques.

For High-FFs, however, some caution is required.

NLP emerged in the 1970s as a radically new approach to psychotherapy and personal change based on, according to the *Oxford English Dictionary* (2009), "a model of interpersonal communication chiefly concerned with the relationship between successful patterns of behaviour and the subjective experiences (esp. patterns of thought) underlying them".

The aim is that awareness of the way both we and others think, speak and behave – and changes in patterns of behaviour and speech based on this awareness – can help people achieve success. NLP has more than a casual link with CBT in this respect, although NLP is CBT on steroids – claiming that adopters can influence the reactions of others to achieve positive external results, rather than simply helping us re-evaluate our responses to external events.

Fine. Yet many NLP practitioners go way beyond understanding thoughts and actions, or even "modelling" the successful behaviour of others. Start researching the claims of the more extreme NLP practitioners and we soon discover offers for rapid and transformational change, with some claiming that wholesale changes can be made in our unconscious mind – including removal of our fears and phobias – almost instantly, even using techniques such as hypnotherapy (and self-hypnosis) in order to achieve this. And with our fears seemingly banished forever, some practitioners also claim that a furious and headlong drive towards "dream fulfilment" is possible.

Of course, such strong claims make NLP both an alluring and potentially dangerous tool in the hands of High-FFs prone to seeking instant change, or to thinking that they can be rewired, or to pursuing inappropriate avoidance-based goals.

NLP needs tempering

While gratefully acknowledging NLP ideas and methodology, therefore, we must remain acutely aware that the stated outcomes from NLP-rooted exercises, including visualisation, may need to be tempered. NLP's critics state that established neuroscience does not support claims regarding the potential for rewiring our self-beliefs, including our fears, meaning that NLP may offer no more than a deeper form of self-denial or perhaps tenuous and refutable "success" through the power of suggestion.

And while I'm not taking sides with respect to NLP's veracity, it is my belief that the moment of realization regarding our faulty wiring, false evaluations and destructive self-belief, is an important one for High-FFs. It needs to be examined and understood – nurtured even. Not swapped for a headlong pursuit in the other direction.

There is no transformational technique that can make that monkey simply disappear. And any attempt at distancing ourselves from him could see him painfully snap back like over-stretched elastic. As High-FFs, we are hardwired to our primary beliefs and default settings, no matter how faulty. They are coming with us I'm afraid, and – in my view – sustainable, long-term progress towards achievement motivation is *only* possible once we realize this and accept it.

Of course, many people who have thought themselves drowning in a sea of insecurities have found strength, purpose and buoyancy through NLP – and that's great (sincerely meant). Yet as a lifeboat NLP can perhaps be compared to Alcoholics Anonymous, with the "recovering" alcoholics having the upper hand in one key respect. They have to reaffirm their addiction at every meeting, meaning they are not permitted any form of self-denial. So while an alcoholic has to introduce themself with the affirmation "my name's [Janet] and I'm an alcoholic", some of those I meet using NLP seem to offer the more proselytising: "my name's [John], and *you* are the insecure one".

This is an important point for the High-FF to grasp, in my opinion. We are "recovering" High-FFs – trying to overcome our insecurities and fears just as alcoholics are trying to overcome their addiction. There is no final victory, just a more promising path and the avoidance of destructive thoughts or behaviour.

And there's a wider point here about anyone using *any* form of self help to improve their lives. Strong short-term progress can lead us into becoming preaching motivational converts – not only seeing insecurities in everyone we meet but offering unsolicited advice. No matter what resources we use for self improvement, we must remember that it is only *our* behaviour that we are seeking to change, not those of our friends or acquaintances – and especially not those of strangers we feel are in need of enlightenment.

Visualization of goals

The above warning on the limits of NLP for High-FFs seeking "recovery" from their fear of failure is necessary simply because of what happens next – the visualization of our goals as so excellently recommended by many of the more professional and enlightened NLP practitioners.

Famous hotelier Conrad Hilton kept a photo of New York's Waldorf Hotel under the glass on his desk. It remained there for 18 years until he bought the hotel. The photo was a daily visual reminder of his goal, giving him the focus he needed to achieve it.

"We are what we are because we have first imagined it," writes Anthony Robbins (1992), adding that setting goals through visualization is the first step in turning the invisible (our future) into the visible.

It certainly worked for me. In my early days as an entrepreneur I organized and attended a seminar at Metrocube, held by one of the UK's leading NLP practitioners. At the seminar she did a curious thing – she made us all close our eyes and imagine ourselves 10 years hence.

For instance, how were we dressed? This is very important as it starts giving an indication about us as people. We were asked to visualize our perfect selves so the assumption was we were well dressed, but in what: summer casuals, a Savile Row suit, the Barbour and wellies of a country squire, or in something from a Paris or Milan catwalk? And who had we become as people? For instance, what is our place of work like? Is it an office in Mayfair, a farmhouse kitchen table, something sleek in a Manhattan skyscraper, or even a workshop under the Brighton railway?

Is it our own company, or are we high up in our target organization (or even just doing the right job in our target organization)? Indeed, can we identify our target organization, as well as the right job?

And who works for us? Is there a team, a partner, a PA, a receptionist, a hierarchy of people below us, or the perfect line manager above? What do they look like? What are *they* wearing in the office?

Perhaps the most important aspect is our home life. Where is our house: Maida Vale, TriBeCa, Alderley Edge, the Cotswolds,

Provence, Sydney? What does it look like? Is it old or new, four storeys or a bungalow, peg-tiled or flat-roofed? Does it have a gravel drive or is it a Belgravia mansion facing on to a square? Is it our only house or are there others? What does it look like inside: the hall, the kitchen, the study, the bedrooms, the bathroom? What is it like outside: acres of lawn and mature trees, a formal garden, a balcony with a cool cityscape view, or maybe a ramshackle farmyard?

And who are we with? Is it our current partner or someone new? Are there kids? If so, how many? What are their names? Dogs, horses, snakes, fish? What are *their* names?

One thing I remember is just how much detail our NLP practitioner sought. We were actually projecting ourselves into our bedroom or office, actually greeting our colleagues and partners, actually stroking the dog and wandering the grounds of our house.

Parcelling up the 10-year goals

There are several versions of visualization. Another imagines speakers at our funeral, although I like the 10-year version (Anthony Robbins also has a 10-year horizon) because it contains lots of detail and – crucially – it allows us to parcel-up the expanse of time in front of us. The 10-year visualization exercise gives us a whole decade to reach our goals. That house, office, career, book and dog does not have to be in place until the end of year 9, month 11, day 30.

However, you do need to take the right steps towards it today. After your 10-year visualization, therefore, an important next task is to visualize where you would have to be in five years to make that 10-year goal achievable. Again, details please – what does every aspect look and feel like? Then what about in two years' time – where would you have to be in 24 months to meet those five-year goals? Again, lots and lots of detail. And what about in 12 months? Where would you have to be to meet the two-year goal? The same goes for six months, then one month, then one week. It is obvious where this ends up. What has to happen tomorrow to meet the one-week goal, and what can be done *now* in preparation for tomorrow's actions?

Lurid fantasies

Yet there's an important caveat to this process. For any "recovering" High-FF aiming to adopt the behaviours of those with high achievement motivation alarm bells should have been ringing during the 10-year visualization exercise as we may have indulged ourselves in the most lurid fantasies imaginable. We are encouraged to "play a role", which means many of us could well have lost ourselves opting for the Beverley Hills mansion with its own recording studio, a guitar-shaped swimming pool and lots of gorgeous and sexually-available people hanging on to our every word.

Despite what many self motivators will say, such fantasies could well be inappropriate goals, not because they are out of reach but because, as High-FFs, we chose them simply because they were, indeed, out of reach. There was no, or little, emotional cost in fantasising at this level because we knew it was never going to happen – at least, short of a major lottery win (see below on the lottery). Such indulgences may well be counterproductive for the recovering High-FF as these are hardly the challenging but achievable and rewarding goals of those with achievement motivation. This, to me, looks like a potentially dangerous encouragement to throw the hoop towards the peg from as far back as possible.

Picking the right jungle

It is worth noting here that this book is not saying "get real" and perhaps end up with a small promotion and one extra bedroom. It is a book aimed at helping those with a high fear of failure to understand what has happened to them and how they can use this knowledge to calculate better responses that help them achieve better results in the future.

If it leads us permanently away from the High-FF prison of negative self-fulfilling responses to the sunlit uplands of achievement motivation then that is a massive, *massive*, success – and one that cannot be measured in guitar-shaped swimming pools. And goal-setting is a vital part of this – *the* most vital part, in fact, as it is about pointing us in the right direction after having spent a lifetime stuck in the wrong place and facing the wrong way thanks to the purgatory of our fears and insecurities.

The most vital action you can take at this point, therefore, is to generate goals that matter to *you*. Goals that are yours – not the fantasies fed to you by marketing men exploiting your vulnerabilities, or by Simon Cowell, Anthony Robbins or any other star maker or guru. Only then will the goals be sustainable and achievable. Only then will you, slowly – over many years – prevent your fear of failure from derailing your progress as, step-by-step, you move towards your goals.

The Character Ethic

Stephen Covey of *Seven Habits* . . . fame is probably the high priest of appropriate goal setting, although his true genius for those with a high fear of failure is that he doesn't ask us to reinvent ourselves or deny our past pain in order to make progress: quite the opposite. He argues against what he calls the "Personality Ethic" prevalent in most modern self-help books and instead promotes the "Character Ethic".

The Personality Ethic, states Covey, relies on developing skills and techniques that can result in quick success. However, these may be revealed as insincere (even manipulative) and will lose their lustre as soon as we hit a major difficulty that the techniques cannot deal with. The Personality Ethic forces us to wear a mask – to display a personality that is inconsistent with our character. Such masks could include the confident, witty or attractive person that the self-help books and techniques are trying to promote – stating that this person is within us and waiting to come out, when in fact we are being asked to express ourselves based on learned or acquired behaviours that are the opposite to our inner selves.

The Character Ethic, meanwhile, is based on developing a character that complements our principles – in fact is "principles-centred". This is a long-term process aimed at bearing fruit according to natural law: i.e., over years (Covey uses a farming analogy of things taking time to propagate and grow). There are *no* short cuts or quick-fixes.

And from our principle-centred character all goals and behaviours flow. We need to develop and explore the principles that provide the blank canvass upon which we draw our map. Covey's call is that we formulate goals based on principles that he claims are innate in human beings: including fairness, integrity, honesty, human dignity, quality and excellence. They also include the idea of human potential, growth and encouragement.

The principles come first

My first reading of this made me hesitate, I have to admit. I was absorbed in a book focused on making me more effective and was instead getting a lecture on ethics and morality. It felt too holy for me, too sanctimonious. Many of the most effective people I have ever met were scoundrels: immorally and unethically pursuing their self-interest with no care for the external consequences (a lack of concern that I secretly admired, so wrapped up was I in what other people thought of me). Certainly, they were not "principles centred". In fact, many were so eaten up with ambition they were deeply unprincipled, although I recognize now that this may have been due to their inner frustrations and insecurities.

But then the penny dropped. I wasn't trying to become one of these people, however much I secretly envied them. I was trying to move away from High-FF behaviour (which many of them displayed) and towards high achievement motivation. I was prepared to accept there were no short cuts to doing this. And having to accept that this involved setting goals that were principles-centred was just another step, which I eventually took.

I realized Covey is right. When I studied myself in depth I didn't find a bad person despite some shamefully spiteful and selfish acts. I found a good person with a burning sense of injustice about how the world had treated me thus far. Those very moments of bad behaviour were based on feelings of frustration, which I had always inwardly justified as such – to the point of feeling shocked and harshly judged when my behaviour had been pulled up by others.

In fact, I had often mused that inside every bad person was a good person trying to get out. Many muggers, bank robbers, even murderers would inwardly justify their actions based on prejudice against them or poor opportunities. Most would see themselves as, at heart, a good person. Certainly, frustration has been a key driver for my bad behaviour over the years. Remove the frustration, I reasoned, and the principle-centred good guy would come forth.

And Covey was simply saying I had this the wrong way round. Being principle-centred means that the hidden good person within needs to come to the fore first in order to act as a benchmark and driver for our new goals and behaviours. We must move towards the person we want to be – emotionally and spiritually – not become that person only once we have arrived at some new destination. In terms of principles, the journey and the destination are one and the same. And they start here.

This was one of those revelatory moments for me. It confirmed two things: that my internal fight between the good and bad me is a crucial battle in my quest to overcome my fear of failure, and that the good person is innate – I had simply developed bad thoughts and behaviours from bad experiences. It also confirmed that the future would be better than the past because I now realized this and could act accordingly – using my principles to act as a strong benchmark for my goal setting, as well as my future behaviour.

I then had another revelation, about the unprincipled people I'd envied. In my careers there had been a few but, looking back, I realized that none of these people had prospered. One had lost his job after arrogantly conducting an affair in the office, another had run his company into the ground after playing fast and loose with his creditors, and then there were my colleagues who found themselves in prison after pleading guilty to fraud-related charges. Just maybe being principle-centred was also the most sustainable way to proceed.

Our own constitution

Having encouraged a principle-centred orientation Covey then states we must use that centre to generate appropriate, long-term and enduring goals. But we first have to write a personal mission statement that includes our values and principles.

Covey invoked the example of the *US Constitution* – a document I studied at university and had admired for its brevity, accuracy and totemic qualities. The *US Constitution* (along with the *Bill of Rights* included within it) encapsulated the principles and values of the new republic and set a very clear standard for future generations to adhere to. Covey wrote that the *US Constitution* made it crystal clear when such standards had been breached: during the Watergate scandal for instance. And such is the grounding of that document that it is my belief that it was an important building block in the creation of the US as a superpower.

So there are clear advantages for creating your own constitution. It is not a document that should be scribbled or hurried, however. Think about it over days and weeks, and add to it over a period of time. Anthony Robbins talks of writing our goals rapidly without pause, which is fine for a first draft. However, *Your Constitution* is something that needs to be honed. You should also consider it the first "action" in your recovery from fear of failure and then commit it to your diary (perhaps in those back pages marked "notes"), which will give you the opportunity to review it annually.

My Constitution (for illustrative purposes only – in my view this is a deeply private document):

- To be a strong mentor and example to my children.
- To honour my marriage vows – that's why I made them.
- To create a career I am proud of.
- To make a difference.
- To create a legacy from the work I do.
- To seek happiness but to accept that happiness comes from within.
- To recognize failings and mistakes and to make amends.
- To recognize that my irritation and impatience with others is not their failing but mine.
- To act with integrity and to honour my debts.
- To not work purely for money.
- To realize that my first reaction is not always the correct one.
- To "never surrender".

Given the above, it is hard to see how being a hotshot investment banker or humorous laddish writer were ever appropriate goals for me to pursue.

And there is an important point here about ambitions. If you genuinely think a key element of *Your Constitution* is "to be rich" or "to be famous" then you should write it. But it may also be worth asking yourself "why?" If the deep and genuine answer is "because I want to drive a Ferrari" or "because I want to be recognized in the street", that's fine. But what if the deep and genuine answer is "to show everyone that I am not worthless"? Then a better line for *Your Constitution* may be "to prove my worth", with more specific objectives consigned to the 10-year visualization. Remember, *Your Constitution* is about developing your principles. It's not about your dream job or what brand of jeans you want to wear in five years' time.

A dynamic towards appropriate goal setting

Your Constitution is aimed at getting you to the next stage: developing specific objectives and milestones – as defined by your principles. Others agree with Covey on this. According to Brian Tracy (2003), our values define us – generating the following dynamic towards appropriate goal setting:

(a) First we discover our values.
(b) We then determine our beliefs from our values.
(c) We derive our attitude from our beliefs.
(d) We arrive at our expectations from our attitudes. And, finally,
(e) We set our actions from our expectations.

If we reverse this chain it is easy to see where things go wrong for the High-FF. Our expectations of failure mean that we set inappropriate goals because of our belief that we are incapable of achievement. This incapacity is derived from our values, which include placing a higher focus on maintaining face than on achievement.

But just say we were to start with more appropriate, principle-based values and then run these through Tracy's dynamic. If a core value was to focus on continual self improvement, our beliefs must be that continuous self improvement is possible, which will surely have a beneficial impact on our attitude towards learning – it is there to help us live by our core values. This attitude fuels positive expectations regarding self improvement and drives our actions.

Suddenly, we are facing the right way with some clear values and principles to achieve and maintain. Project these forward and we can indulge ourselves in those NLP visualizations to help us define our goals in detail.

Goal-setting may take several goes

And if, by the end of all these exercises, you do not have a well-thought-through and achievable action plan for the next 10 years, then you need to go back to *Your Constitution* and think again about your principles and values. This is nothing to beat yourself up about. It may take several goes. And realizing that the goals need resetting at this stage is a lot less painful than realizing this five years down the line (although be aware that goals may, can and should change).

Your actions now are based on putting the ladder against the right wall, so answers may not be instant. The visualization may take a few goes, as may *Your Constitution*. That's fine. You have a lifetime to get this right (with the first 10 years your immediate focus) and the journey is likely to be a lot nicer than the painful and bumpy ride you have so far experienced.

What's Stopping You? *Visualizing your desired destination 10 years hence is a strong starting point for goal-setting – especially when then divided into milestones that connect now with then. But avoiding inappropriate goal-setting requires you to first develop* Your Constitution *based on your principles and values.*

7

LANGUAGE AND BEHAVIOUR

The point of all this goal-setting activity is, of course, to generate proactivity. And a key element of proactive behaviour is proactive language.

"The right words can have a galvanising effect, generating enthusiasm, energy, momentum and more, while the wrong words can undermine the best intentions and kill initiative on the spot, stone dead," writes leadership guru Stephen Denning in *The Secret Language of Leadership* (2007).

Whether it is *Your Constitution*, your goal-setting, your diary, or simply your thoughts and words, you need to adopt the right tone and vocabulary.

Covey (1989) points out that reactive language is based on absolving us – "that's just the way I am", "there's nothing I can do" and so on. It is saying "I'm not responsible", "I was born this way".

But you *are* responsible. You were not born this way. You became this way through your own responses and behaviours, whatever the external root causes. In fact, you became this way partly because of the language you used. Reactive or defeatist language is – like fear itself – self-fulfilling.

Write down your goals

Luckily there is a major opportunity to put this right. Having been through the goal-setting visualization exercises you now need to write them down. And while writing them down is an opportunity to re-evaluate your goals and ensure they make sense – that the one year is connected to the two-year and so on up to the 10-year summit – they are also an opportunity to adopt the right tone and language.

This is not rocket science. For instance, you should write the goals in present-tense language. Lindsey Agness (2008) states that we should behave as if we are already there – that our goals have already been achieved – which also holds true for the language we use when writing our goals. For instance, if we make the journey as certain as a train ride we are compelled to take the steps that propel us forward.

"We arrive at Manchester Piccadilly Station at 16:45," says the announcer on the *Virgin* train.

"Year 10: we are living in a self-built six-bedroom house in Norfolk with three horses, two dogs and a rare breed of sheep."

Are we? *Wow* – have we named all the sheep yet?

Goals need to be that specific, involving – according to Julie Starr, MD of Starr Counselling in *The Coaching Manual* (2002) – the what, where, when and whom.

"I want more energy," is too vague, she states, and therefore less motivating than "I want more energy to be able to play sports with my kids after work."

Add the timescale (each week), venue (at the new leisure centre) and the sport (badminton) and the objective is just one phone call and a quick trip to a sports shop (probably located within the leisure centre) from being converted into sustainable action.

Behave as if we are already there

According to Lindsey Agness, the process of "behaving as if you are already there" and using language that supports this contention is an important one because it produces new more positive neural pathways in the brain. And these are built upon with each positive step in the right direction. We cannot aim at achievement motivation and continue to behave in ways dictated by our fear of failure. If necessary, we have to "fake it 'til we make it" to use the expression of many self-help writers, most notably Tom Bay and David Macpherson in *Change Your Attitude* (1998).

If you want to be promoted, they suggest, you have to act as if you already have been – taking on the airs of the seniors around you, adopting their seriousness and dropping the office clown persona that may have been a mask for your disappointments. Over time this will become an unconscious habit and will become noticed by those in the hierarchy above you.

Obviously there may be limits to this. The Norfolk farm in year 10 is a strong goal but turning up to work in our green wellies may raise a few eyebrows. Spending the weekend in wellies scouring Norfolk for the perfect location, on the other hand, is fine – especially if, like Conrad Hilton, we then keep a photo of it on our desk.

Having said this, your goal-centred behaviours are necessarily different from your behaviours as a High-FF. You may find that the behavioural traits that chained you to the floor (such as clowning) are the very traits that made you popular with particular people (often fellow High-FFs). These traits have to change, for sure – but there is no need to change your friends. You could instead add to *Your Constitution* "to radiate positivity".

Positive self-talk

Negative self-talk also has to go, to be replaced with positive self-talk.

According to John Caunt (2003) you should cut yourselves some slack – questioning negative thoughts and opinions and recognising instead your positive qualities, even writing down (in the usual place) strong statements of support that help recast your set beliefs and reframe your outlook using "half full" rather than "half empty" language.

In *Change Your Attitude*, Bay and Macpherson implore us to overcome the negative self-talk, stating that everyone has inbuilt negative self-talk tapes they need to destroy. Instead, we should learn to compliment ourselves, they state, which is true at every level – even if you are simply recording those small but accumulating achievements in your diary.

And goals should be stated in positive terms, moving towards what you want rather than what you don't want. Aims such as "I don't want to be poor" are meaningless, they state, and should be replaced with positive and more specific statements such as "I want to be able to afford the four bedroom house in that leafy neighbourhood I've always coveted". Explore why you want *that* house, and you're probably getting closer still to a more constitutional assessment of what really motivates you.

Yet all this positive talk must not lead us into a false paradigm. The words used have to be authentically yours or you will be fooling yourself. How can you tell? Not easy, especially in the early days when our "natural state" seems to come with such a negative dialogue. Injecting positive language into such a pessimistic outlook feels like walking back into a stadium as the fans pour out after the final whistle.

Wait a little longer, however, and the crowds are gone. Go back into the stadium and you can shout what you like and it will echo off the rafters. And by writing down your goals you are giving yourself that space to turn around your thinking, as well as change your language from negative to positive. You are deliberately no longer part of the crowd and you can adopt what language you like.

However, positive next steps that are written and then ignored perhaps need to be examined. Is there a reason you have not enrolled onto that language or accountancy course? Maybe your desire to learn Japanese or qualify as an accountant is something that has been fed to you from elsewhere. Maybe it was never *your* goal in the first place, and an art foundation course or small business enterprise scheme would be far more motivating.

Pre- and post-visualization exercises

Goal-setting is harder work than it first appears and requires time and soul searching, although there are many pre-visualization exercises you can try if you are struggling to set appropriate goals.

One comes from Jim Cairo in *Motivation and Goal Setting* (1998), who states that the importance of setting goals that are consistent with your true identity is vital as these goals will sustain your motivation over time. And if you are struggling with determining your true self (a common problem for recovering High-FFs). Cairo suggests ranking the following attributes 1 to 10 in importance:

- Security
- Wealth
- Good health
- Relationship with partner
- Relationship with kids
- Relationship with family
- Fame
- Job/career
- Power
- Happiness
- Friendship
- Retirement
- Owning your own business
- Long life
- Travel
- Respect of peers
- Spiritual fulfilment
- Charity

What are the highest-ranking attributes? These should get 80 percent of your time and form a basis for your goal setting, says Cairo. And they can feed into *Your Constitution*, which remains your key grounding document for goal-setting.

And there are post goal-setting exercises we can employ to ensure we are on the right path. Lindsey Agness (2008) quotes well-known success guru Paul J. Meyer who recommends the mnemonic SMART when assessing our goal-setting. According to Meyer, our objectives should be:

* Specific (not "lose weight" but "lose 10 pounds")
* Measurable ("lose 10 pounds by June")
* Achievable (i.e., within the bounds of possibility – travel to Mars, for instance, may be a few generations hence)
* Realistic (maybe a half marathon is more realistic this year, with a full marathon next year)
* Timed ("June" it is).

Yet care is needed with measurable objectives – especially those that are time-related. If your aim is to be CEO within a year, changing course on day 365 may be self-defeating. As Anthony Robbins states, many people give up their goals having passed a time-related deadline without realizing they were within days of achieving them. Certainly, being too strict with time horizons can be self-defeating.

The Reticular Activating System – our "antennae"

What is not necessary at this stage is detail on how the goals will be achieved. Mike Dooley, "dream fulfilment" guru and author of *Notes from the Universe* (2007), calls these the "dreaded hows". Dooley's view is that there are a million ways to achieve something, so it is crazy to establish now the how for a goal three years hence.

The secret to "manifesting change", he states, is not focusing on the how but on the desired end result. This seems to chime with just about everybody else I've read on this, although a key additional point he makes is that once we are truly focused on our desired end result "the universe will conspire on our behalf".

In fact, it's not the universe that conspires in our favour once we have cleared the path in front of us to focus on our goals: it is us. Our Reticular Activating System (RAS) does the work. This is the area of the brain responsible for regulating arousal. It is composed of several neuronal circuits connecting the brainstem to the cortex.

No, this didn't mean much to me either – at least not until I realized the RAS is what I used to call "my antennae" – the element of my consciousness that seems to notice things that I am currently focused on. For instance, I was given a Burberry scarf for Christmas. It is lovely, and I have worn it every day so far this winter. Yet since Christmas I have noticed these scarves everywhere on the streets of London – on professionals walking to work, students going to college, day-trippers in Oxford Street.

Why had I not noticed these scarves before? Because my RAS was only alerted to them on Christmas Day when I opened my mother's gift. Only since then has it bothered to draw my attention to just how many of these scarves are out there. Previously my brain had filtered out the scarves, like 99.9 percent of the information it receives, because they meant nothing to me.

For those with a high fear of failure, our RAS has picked up mostly negative stimuli until now. For instance, if we assume there is prejudice against us, the RAS seeks it out (and inevitably finds it). Yet if we focus on our goals – especially ones with the next steps laid out in front of us – anything relevant that passes our senses, sticks. And that's a lot of information. I've often heard people be amazed at the right solution or the right person or the right idea appearing as if from nowhere at exactly the right moment. Yet they hadn't appeared from nowhere. Our RAS found them when they had previously gone unnoticed.

Luck and the winner's curse

One last point on this. The more I read about our RAS the more it occurs to me that it may also have an impact on luck – that key ingredient that those with high achievement motivation seem to have in abundance and us High-FFs seem to lack. Certainly, I have always considered myself unlucky – to the point where I would joke about the "Kelsey Effect" on any company, car, girlfriend, house, street, city or country I alighted upon. Bad things would immediately and unexpectedly start happening to them. And my wife likes to joke about the "Kelsey Cloud" that always seems to follow us on our summer holidays (we even had rain on our trip to the Sahara Desert!).

Yet I noticed that my "luck" seemed to change when I became focused on a particular goal, at least with respect to that goal. Opportunities would appear at the right moment and obstacles disappear. And this I now realize was not luck at all: it was my RAS.

There are also positives to feeling unlucky. I have always hated gambling because of my poor "luck", but now consider this a blessing. Gambling seems to me to be the "winner's curse" – the arrogance of the "lucky" making them over-estimate purely mathematical probabilities. More often than not, gambling results in the most rapid levelling of the "lucky" and the "unlucky" known to man. Thank heavens – and my own High-FF status – that I've avoided that fate.

This extends even to the lottery, which I have never "played" and would beg any recovering High-FF to stop playing. Not only is it a "tax on the stupid" as one clever friend described it, the lottery offers an excuse for inaction when there is no excuse for inaction.

"When I win the lottery," makes me cringe every time I hear it. It's not the lottery that will change your life. It's you.

Assuming poor luck has also led me towards a hatred of "winging it" in meetings and presentations. I am consistently the best briefed and prepped, precisely because I assumed I had to make amends for my poor luck.

Certainly, I have assumed the odds were stacked against me in just about any walk of life, which has, over the years, led to things working out more and more in my favour. As a young person, the cocky assurance of many High-AMs is an obvious advantage when it comes to winning the girl/boy or convincing employers to give them that first break. But life is a marathon, not a sprint, and luck will inevitably go against those relying on that most ephemeral of qualities. Meanwhile, I assumed poor luck from the start, which has prepared me well for the inevitable puddles – many of which I can now deftly sidestep.

What's Stopping You? *Positive language is important when goal-setting, as is "behaving as if you are already there". Yet while your goals have to be detailed, you should avoid focusing on the "dreaded hows" – not least because your RAS will help you once you are heading in the right direction.*

8

APPROPRIATE GOAL-SETTING FOR RECOVERING HIGH-FFS

B ut have we got the right goals? This remains a core concern for those with a high fear of failure because, while keen to avoid near-peg under-achieving, we have a flawed capacity to differentiate our genuine long-term objectives (which we may still be formulating) from inappropriate High-FF "reach for the stars" long-peg dreams that may be an elaborate form of avoidance.

In his book *Destructive Goal Pursuit* (2006), behaviourist D. Christopher Kayes examines inappropriate goal-setting by recounting the story of the 1996 Mount Everest expedition that ended with eight people dead and others requiring amputations. Kayes's claim is that the expedition was flawed from the start due to its goals, which involved expert mountaineers leading a group of mixed-ability adventurers who had paid up to US$65,000 to be there. The commercial status of the expedition changed the dynamic of the climb, he states, because many of the climbers believed they were hiring experts who would ensure they achieved their dream of conquering the mountain.

Kayes blamed the disaster on the relentless pursuit of the goal to conquer the summit even after the experienced team leaders could have heeded warning signs that they were running out of time for a safe descent – a phenomenon Kayes called "goalodicy" (i.e., the pursuit of idiotic goals).

Goalodicy has six key characteristics, states Kayes, many of which will be familiar to High-FFs:

* A narrowly defined goal (to get to the summit).
* Public expectation (these were ambitious people – including a celebrity writer – concerned about how they were perceived both within and beyond the group).
* Face-saving behaviour (from both the climbers and the leaders who might have ignored danger signals in order to maintain their credibility).
* A dream of an idealized future (of conquering Everest).
* Goal-driven justification (if the goal becomes "everything" it can be used to justify irrational decisions that may be dangerous).
* A sense of destiny.

"Goalodicy works by allowing teams to put off the reality of the present in the hope that achieving a future goal will eliminate current obstacles," writes Kayes.

Once a team sets a goal, persuading it otherwise can be difficult, states Kayes. And it can be the same for individuals. Goals pull people through and offer a sense of purpose. Yet setting goals that are way too ambitious or ill-considered against what is actually achievable may inspire more risk taking and make us feel justified in going beyond accepted norms, which can lead to dangerous and even unethical behaviour.

With respect to the Everest climbers, this led to an inability to learn and change as the facts changed around them (their ascent was delayed by bottlenecks and bad weather, which restricted their scope for a safe descent). Their goal was too tight and they were too dependent on one aspect of the pursuit – their leaders, who the followers depended upon as the only people capable of making knowledge-based decisions on whether it was safe to continue.

Setting the wrong goals can be fatal

So what can be learned from Christopher Kayes's excellent recounting of this fated Everest expedition? A key lesson has to be that the team set the wrong goal, despite the fact the goal appeared obvious. That US$65,000 fee was not for an ascent to the summit of Everest. It was for reaching the summit and making it down again – *alive*! It may have been that crucial narrowing of the goal that led to the disaster because it clouded the judgement of the team leaders, who may have become overly concerned about the implicit promises within the fee. And if this sounds unrealistic – that the revised goal is too wide – compare it to the Apollo moon landings, which had getting the astronauts home as an equal and integral objective (just ask Gene Kranz).

An important point here is that progress for its own sake is not progress, despite the fact it may temporarily energize us. If you are working towards the wrong goal, you are simply setting yourself a trap, which – as in the case of the Everest climbers – can lead to a fatal reckoning. At the very least you are simply wasting your time.

Setting the right goals requires us to return to *Our Constitution*. For instance, my goal of a Norfolk farm and a rare breed of sheep looks pretty hollow without my commitments as a father and husband (or as a farmer, which are absent – suggesting it may not even be *my* goal). If I fail to include my family, a lonely farm in the middle of nowhere is probably the last place I'd like to end up.

You have to make sure that your goals are in balance with the rest of your life. As Julie Starr (2003) states, if you want a job with lots of travel and you have a young family, you need to think through the consequences of achieving that goal. If you are prepared to pay that price, fine. But goal-setting based on achievement motivation needs to maintain us through a timeframe that looks well beyond desperate short-term wins that require such an acute level of sacrifice that we end up spending the rest of our lives rueing the day we achieved them. That 10-year time horizon is there for a reason.

Money's diminishing returns

Money is a particular problem when trying to set appropriate goals. Wealth is an obvious objective but perspective is required. In *Living the 80/20 Way* (2005) entrepreneur Richard Koch writes that most people overestimate the return they will receive from earning more. Studies show that poverty makes us unhappy, writes Koch, but once we're moderately well off, adding even more money doesn't make us happier and can even add stresses that get in the way of happiness.

Money-based goals also bring other problems – not dissimilar to those faced on Everest. If your goal is to be a millionaire by the time you are 30, what price are you prepared to pay to achieve it? Perhaps you'll sacrifice a social life and put off any relationship or family commitments. You may even be prepared to be a bit of a toady in the office. But are you prepared to shaft the guy in the next cubicle? You are? OK, what about commit fraud? Really – blimey! So where does it end? Robbery, murder, genocide?

Is there no limit to what you'd do to reach that goal? This is the extreme end of High-FF behaviour – the land of the megalomaniac who is so afraid of failure they are willing to go way beyond inappropriate goal setting. Such extremists will find their own constitution, if written honestly, a document dripping with clenched hatred and perceived injustice (Hitler's *Mein Kampf* is a classic example).

Anthony Robbins (1992) warns against abusing ourselves in the pursuit of a single goal – tying our entire level of personal happiness to our ability to achieve goals that may be beyond our control. It is not just achieving the objective that matters but the quality of life we experience along the way, he says.

Robbins is convinced that many of us go through life putting off our happiness in order to achieve that next goal. "Someday" seems to be the goal of the permanently unhappy, he says. Yet we should decide to be happy now. Goal setting is not some form of delayed gratification. It is about setting our "compass" – as Covey would say – and being uplifted as we start to walk in the right direction, knowing where we are heading and with the faith to deal with the bends in the road along the way.

"Remember the direction we are heading is more important than the individual results," says Robbins.

Setting goals beyond our goals

Another core component of this is in having goals beyond our goals. One of the key reasons I failed at both investment banking and as a writer is that I had no idea what to do once I'd "made it". I'd not thought about the next stage at all, meaning that I floundered within both roles without any of the focus and drive that won me the opportunities in the first place.

"Never give up setting goals," says Robbins. "Achieving our goals can be a curse unless we have already set higher goals before reaching the first."

The idea of "outrunning" our dreams, as I found out at the bank, can lead to an "is that all" deflation, albeit in a better setting. Lindsey Agness (2008) quotes John Grinder (the co-founder of NLP) stating that the biggest factor stopping goal achievement is often the failure to set goals beyond our initial goal. With no higher level to aim for we can end up sabotaging ourselves the minute the original goal is achieved – exactly what happened to me with both banking and writing.

Hopefully, setting 10-year goals that complement *Your Constitution* – including short-term milestones – should help overcome this problem. *Your Constitution* should create a framework for both your short-term objectives and long-term ambitions. For instance, Julie Starr's parent wanting energy to play sport with her kids would soon find the badminton sessions losing their appeal unless she could take it to the next stage. Perhaps her real objective was to "stay connected and relevant to my children as they move from childhood to adulthood". As a part of *Her Constitution* it would make the badminton sessions just one part of a programme with a clearly-defined, long-term objective that also contains flexibility and a measurable result.

Importantly, such a statement also avoids being a hostage to fortune – such as becoming a millionaire by 30 or summiting Everest at the first attempt. Of those that perished on Everest, surely a better objective would have been "to become an accomplished mountaineer" or even the more constitutional "to maintain my sense of physical adventure throughout my life".

If we could have our goals now – would we?

Another way of checking whether we are heading in the right direction is to adopt another one of Julie Starr's methodologies from *The Coaching Manual*. If you could have your goal now, she asks, would you take it? If there are any caveats to prevent you immediately and whole-heartedly shouting "*YES*", you may need to examine why this is the case.

If, for instance, you visualized yourself running a company of 100 people and – offered the opportunity to do so – hesitate or even panic at the thought, it may be that such a goal is no more than a fantasy (perhaps given to you by someone else or by conditioning). Maybe a goal more tailored to your wellbeing would be running a smaller team of, say, five, but in a collegiate studio setting, maybe in a town with a more human scale.

Of course, the 100-person company may well be appropriate as a 10-year goal after a good baptism of fire involving a company with fewer employees. Having said this, your terror at the thought of running such a company now should also have an impact on your 10-, five- or two-year goals, and even on *Your Constitution*.

We need to concentrate on being who *we* are. Most of the Everest climbers were not professional mountaineers – many were disastrously ill-prepared for climbing a mountain that was climbed for the first time *ever* only in 1953 (at least officially).

"If you have a lemon, make lemonade," wrote Dale Carnegie (1948), meaning we should look at what we have and what we can do with it.

This is not advocating that changes in direction are ill-advised. It is simply stating that aiming to become a mathematics professor when it is obvious we are more of the creative-writer type will massively increase our chances of failure and further disappointment. And that will reinforce rather than counter our negative self-beliefs.

Recognize the milestones

A final element that can scupper the progress we make from goal setting is in becoming so caught up in the process of goal achievement that we fail to observe how far we have come. Progress can creep up on us to the point where we ignore it, which means we maintain the negative feelings we had before we started and fail to look at past achievements as building blocks for the future. This is a crucial failing of the High-FF and can result in our progress towards our goals having no impact on our general wellbeing. In some respects this is inevitable – we are who we are. Those neural hijackings are not going to disappear.

However, just as we can learn to refute the hijackings more and more quickly, so we can learn – over time – that the feelings we have are false and that those tiny steps of progress towards our goals should start to build our confidence and reduce our fears. Of course, keeping a diary helps, as does the annual renewal of *Your Constitution* and your goals. Indeed, if your goals roll forward you are always 10 years from achieving them, which could be frustrating unless you also recognize that you are constantly meeting milestones that are both confirming and confidence-building. We just need to make sure that we recognize the milestones for what they are and note the small victories as we win them – perhaps with a big tick in the diary.

What's Stopping You? *You need to ensure that your goals complement who you are. You also need goals beyond your initial goals. And you need to recognize the progress you make along the way.*

PART THREE
Execution

9

STRATEGY AND TACTICS

Objectives, strategy, tactics. That's our order at Moorgate when planning a PR campaign. And it seems perfectly applicable as a route for execution when developing achievement motivation in individuals with a high fear of failure. So with the objectives written, we need to move to the next stage: establishing our "strategy" for execution, although this immediately presents us with a problem. What – exactly – is a strategy?

The dictionary definition states it is the "art or science of the planning and conduct of a war," which is helpful but too broad for me and, I suspect, many recovering High-FFs. We can be easily put off by ambiguities, with even the meaning of a word sometimes enough to halt our progress. And while many books have been written with the word "strategy" in the title, nearly all assume an understanding of the word and then promptly mix strategy and tactics without any recognition of their different roles in the pursuit of our goals.

"In order for a goal to be attainable, it must be *operationally defined*," says Phillip C. McGraw, the author of *Life Strategies* (1999), which seemed the most obvious self-help book to consult because it was aimed at individuals rather than businesses.

The italics on "operationally defined" are mine because it jumped out at me as a possible definition of strategy, although – again – an operational definition could become confused with the practical day-to-day tactics and action points we employ.

The strategic bridge

After toying with this conundrum for a while I realized that, even in our PR campaigns, we tend to use the "strategy" section of our Campaign Plan – our key execution document that gives the client confidence regarding our aims for the campaign and the steps we are taking to achieve them – as a chance to summarize the objectives before translating them into relevant tactics and action points. In other words, the strategy bridges the client's goals and our actual actions – ensuring that our tactics (i.e., the executable action points) are focused on meeting the objectives. And this, to me, is the perfect definition of a strategy.

Strategies are not always obvious

As a bridge between the objectives and the executable tactics, the strategy is therefore vital. For military planners trying to achieve their objective (victory), one strategy could be to execute "total war" – attacking by land, sea and air. This may seem like an obvious strategy in war, but it isn't. Alternative strategies could be to wait for an opponent's onslaught or operate a guerrilla campaign in enemy territory (yet even here we can see tactical language slipping in). So a strategy of "total war" may lead, tactically, to the employment of company A – backed up by warship B and air squadron C – to storm beach X in month Y.

At Moorgate we have found that settling on a strategy for the client can be the most difficult part of a campaign – not least because it can seem so obvious at the start. Obvious strategies – like winning a war using the army, navy and air force – can result in objectives melding into tactics too readily, with potentially disastrous results.

For instance, a common objective in public relations is to generate warm sales leads for our clients. Most clients assume that such an objective translates into a strategy of generating news coverage via tactics such as writing and distributing a series of news releases before lobbying for coverage in a particular press segment. But is such a strategy correct? Well that depends on the client. If our client is a challenger in the sector, perhaps just launching new services aimed at a particular group, then a strategy of building public profile by generating news articles over a period of months will surely work best.

But what if the client has long-standing expertise and is fending off the challengers? Perhaps the strategy here should be to profile their track-record, which would encourage tactics such as writing opinion-pieces or profile articles, or maybe case studies of happy clients or completed projects. In both scenarios the tactics employed are very much a product of a strategy developed to suit the client's strengths (and weaknesses), which differ greatly despite the identical objective.

This is important because, as Steven Silbiger says in *The 10 Day MBA* (1993), "strategic plans cannot be formed in a vacuum. They must fit organizations just as marketing plans must be suited to products," which is in line with our need as individuals to undertake a campaign for progress that takes account of our strengths and weaknesses.

Advantages of a strategy

Certainly, there are benefits to having a strategy, as outlined by Robert S. Kaplan in *The Execution Premium* (2008):

"Strategic initiatives represent the force that accelerates an organizational mass [or individual] into action, overcoming inertia and resistance to change," making the strategy the key element for injecting momentum into our pursuits.

Indeed, in *Life Strategies* McGraw points out that having a strategy frees us from a "pointless and misguided reliance on willpower", which he considers a myth – "an unreliable emotional fuel, experienced at fever pitch".

Willpower will temporarily energize our efforts, he says – helping us to make the leap – but it will also bring us to a halt once the emotional responses to our early progress have dissipated. This makes willpower a dangerous energizer for High-FFs too used to being driven by their emotions and insecurities. Far better, says McGraw, to develop and execute a well-defined strategy – especially one that manages to remove our emotions as key drivers.

And Kaplan and Silbiger's references to organizations point to another strength of having a strategy – our chance to depersonalize our goal-seeking endeavours. As stated in Part One, this is not about us as people. It is about us achieving our goals, which stand outside of any judgement about who we are. Depersonalization allows us to think of ourselves as companies – as *Me Inc.* – which means we are focused on achieving our objectives by developing a strategy and employing suitable tactics rather than focused on our concerns regarding how our actions look to outsiders. Such a focus clearly aids our judgement because we are no longer interpreting every bump in the road as a personal and final verdict, which also prevents setbacks from sabotaging our decision-making.

The strength of adopting "objectives, strategy, tactics"

Sorry to labour the point, but outlining a strategy offers one final strength. As stated, at Moorgate we execute PR campaigns after first recording the strategy on a Campaign Plan that also contains the objectives, tactics and – as we are a PR company – the audiences and messages. The client then agrees all this and we execute. Yet if our tactics do not produce the desired results we can work our way back up the document, first questioning and replacing the tactics while assuming the strategy fine. Then, if this fails, we can reassess whether we have the right strategy, and finally we can re-evaluate the objectives.

We therefore have a structural confidence that allows us to execute without any nagging doubts regarding the achievability of the objective, which is put in its place at the very top of our Campaign Plan. Only after repeated tactical failures do we look at the strategy. And only after repeated strategic failures would we begin to question the achievability of the objectives.

There is a tremendous strength in recovering High-FFs adopting such as approach. Tactical failures are simply action points that failed to produce the desired result. Yet so many High-FFs interpret even minor setbacks as affirmation of their inner and irretrievable awfulness. Not only is this patently untrue – a conclusion based purely on perception (although a potentially self-fulfilling one) – such a conclusion is impossible if we have, first, depersonalized our goals as part of a *Me Inc.* project and, second, divorced our strategy and tactics from our objectives so that setbacks in execution do not derail our progress towards our goals.

The war *will* be won. It is just a question of how.

The SWOT

So how do we determine the right strategy? As stated, we must tailor our strategy to our strengths and weaknesses, so these need to be assessed. One method we use for our clients is to first undertake a SWOT (strengths, weaknesses, opportunities, threats) analysis, which we add to the Campaign Plan. SWOTs are also advocated by Harvard Business School, no less. Its book *Strategy* (2005), which again invokes the war analogy – states that even the best battle plan is useless unless commanders understand whether their soldiers can carry it out. And this needs to take strengths and limitations into account.

From the SWOT we usually find that the strategy becomes clear, as it will tell us about our readiness for execution, our knowledge regarding the resources required and whether we have those resources to hand. It will also alert us to issues that may arise to destabilize us, as well as alternative tactics we can employ or consider employing – perhaps being opportunistic (previously the realm of the High-AM).

Again, this can work for individuals as well as companies. Certainly it worked for me when I set up Moorgate. My strategy needed to take account of the fact I had not one jot of PR experience and knew no one in the PR industry, but that I had strong journalistic skills and "good" experience in banking.

The objective was obvious – to create a successful financial PR agency starting with the major banks (the entities I best understood) as clients. But what then? I did a SWOT analysis and it was from this that the obvious strategy emerged, albeit one that would have remained hidden without such an exercise.

It went something like this:

Strengths
- A strong background in financial journalism and magazine editing.
- "Good" experience in banking – especially corporate and investment banking (UK/US).
- Lots of contacts in banking and financial journalism.
- Some experience in entrepreneurialism.
- A strong desire to stop failing at things.

Weaknesses
- No actual PR experience, or track record.
- US-experience meant my London contact base was old.
- Lack of self-belief has been my historical undoing.
- Other multiple debilitating insecurities caused by a negative and persistent monkey residing on my back.

Opportunities
- As an editor I remember being irritated by ill-informed PRs – surely a well-informed PR would get a better response?

- Many big PR agencies court the banks but neglect corporate banking, despite the size of that market. This is partly because of its complexity – it is aimed at highly-sophisticated financial directors.

- This neglect has left many corporate bankers doing their own PR – including me when I was a banker (so, in fact, I do have some PR experience – I'd just discounted it). But most bankers find it a pain and don't know if they are PR-ing themselves correctly. They need help.

- I am in a strong position to start an agency because I ran an incubator for start-ups, which is being sold.

Threats
- The incubator may close before I have time to establish Moorgate.
- Rivals may catch on and do it themselves – especially given that our target clients will all have currently-contracted PR agencies.
- I may hate it.
- The monkey may win.

A strategy based on strengths and opportunities

So the obvious strategy emerged – focus on my former area of corporate banking using my strong journalistic skills as bait for those now struggling to execute their own PR. And the fact I had no track record in PR was irrelevant given my other experiences – in fact, given how poorly the existing PR agencies had performed in this area, it was an advantage.

A clear weakness, however, was my eroded contact base – a major failing for a PR. Yet having identified this as a weakness, I was able to direct my early tactics in that direction. I contacted the few people I still knew in London and wangled meetings just to discuss the PR idea. I also accepted any offer to attend conferences or drinks parties and, importantly, kept networking after half the people I spoke to raised an eyebrow regarding my plans and excused themselves. Half the room didn't, so I focused on them, especially the banker who started complaining about having to do his own marketing – including writing articles for English language magazines despite being Dutch.

Finally I read any online (i.e., free) material I could find and searched for people in corporate banking busily PR-ing themselves. I would then make contact, being careful to compliment their PR skills while suggesting I could extend their range.

In fact the SWOT led to one tactical mistake – which it could have also prevented had I paid it proper attention. The lack of contacts, and my specialist knowledge, fooled me into thinking I could approach other PR agencies and suggest a "white label" service for them to offer their existing clients. So focused was I on blind activity that I emailed a dozen or so agencies asking for a meeting and, of course, those that were to become my closest rivals were more than happy for me to reveal my plan for wrestling business away from them.

Had I known more about the PR industry I would have known that – like male Siamese Fighting Fish – no two agencies can ever be in the same room without trying to kill each other, which means handing over intellectual property to the competition is potentially suicidal. Yet my closest rivals failed to see how they were underserving the sector so didn't change their behaviour – meaning they didn't catch on to the potential of our methodology until Moorgate was well established.

Be different

Of course, without realizing it I'd hit upon a key strategic concept when starting a business: differentiation – a concept that works just as well for individuals.

"Specialization lines up where the world is going," says renowned corporate strategist Jack Trout in his book *Trout on Strategy* (2004), stating that we should offer a key "point of differentiation" from others (including our peers) to establish our brand in the customer's (or our boss's) mind.

What are the trends in our area or targeted area, including our career or company? Where is that world heading? What is done badly? Why? How can it be improved? What are the barriers to this improvement? What role can *we* play? Do we want that role? If yes, what's our strategy for achieving this?

But differentiation requires self-belief, especially when – as in my case – half the people we approach think we are crazy (often those with the most experience in a particular area). Yet experience executing PR as a banker – as well as my misguided meetings with other agencies – gave me the self-belief to realize my detractors didn't matter. In fact, they were the ones that persuaded me of the gap in the market for financial PR that didn't involve blond bobs, dazzle-white teeth and flirty smiles (none of which I possess).

Actually, I was grateful for their presence as they provided a strong benchmark for my differentiation. I could turn what I was not into a positive. Indeed, Steve Chandler (2001) encourages us to "exploit our weaknesses".

We should turn the traits, tendencies and characteristics we most dislike about ourselves into signature assets, he says, citing Arnold Schwarzenegger who used his Austrian accent as a selling point for the movies and being a political outsider as a vote winner for politics.

The "jumping out of the aeroplane" moment

With the strategy decided we can move towards tactical execution – actually storming beach X in month Y. Researching the market for the right organization to work for is a tactic, a job application is a tactic, developing a contact base in a particular industry is a tactic. Tactics are our immediate action points towards meeting our goals – often clustered under various headings such as relationship building, skill acquisition or research. They represent a big moment. This is the recovering High-FF's equivalent of jumping out of the aeroplane and no amount of instruction, training and parachute-checking is going to take away the terror of that moment.

In fact, the preparation *is* our parachute. It will allow us to act – not least because in developing our strategy the next steps should appear logical if not obvious. An important point of principle here is that we must do what feels like the most logical next step. Have faith that the seemingly obvious thing to do is almost certainly the right next move – not least because it will be the product of all that planning. This is the moment we pull the lever on our machine, so the widget that comes out the bottom should, of course, look familiar.

"Simplicity is the first principle."

At least that's the advice of Sun Tzu's *Art of War*, as applied to business in *Sun Tzu for Execution* by US entrepreneur and Sun Tzu enthusiast Steven W. Michaelson (2007). "If execution is more complicated than it needs to be it won't be as successful," he writes, while ". . . simple ideas, executed with gusto, have a tendency to work. And they work despite their shortcomings."

It doesn't take long for most business books that discuss tactics to start quoting this famous Chinese war-focused philosopher. Yet Michaelson's is an excellent application of Sun Tzu's philosophy because it focuses on execution. For instance, he states that size is unimportant – "the battle doesn't always go to the side with the biggest army" – while preparation is key, as is seizing a favourable position beforehand – "for Sun Tzu a favourable position gave control over the battlefield". Attitude is also important – "a positive attitude wins over a negative one" – as is speed – "speed is the essence of war" and opportunism – "if the enemy leaves a door open, you must rush in".

The required fight

Sun Tzu – especially as translated by Michaelson – can put fire in our bellies for the battles ahead. But it may not work for everyone, especially as many High-FFs have poor experience of battles. Those with a high fear of failure often "retire hurt" from such fights feeling as if they have been tactically outmanoeuvred and physically outgunned, probably by someone who spends their evenings reading Sun Tzu. Indeed, going back to those Atkinson-style experiments, battles are the very thing High-FFs hate most, making battle analogies offputting when it comes to motivation.

Yet we are our own worst enemy in this respect. We are trying to beat our inner demons to make progress in our lives. And this requires fight. We cannot be pacifists in this endeavour. We *will* face external competition, whatever our goals. There are many applicants for every promotion or job, many companies vying for the business of our potential clients, many rivals for the attentions of our intended personal conquests. And we have rolled over too many times already in our lives.

Giving way to the High-AM because, what the hell, they were bound to win in the end, is no longer a viable option. It is self-fulfilling defeatism that has no place in the thinking of a recovering High-FF. This is the point where we make our stand. So there is no escaping the fact we have a battle on our hands (although, as we shall see, not all battles involve a win : lose outcome). And, in this respect, Sun Tzu seems pretty apt in helping us mentally prepare.

Rules for tactical execution

If we are therefore reconciled to battle, how do we align our forces and move onwards to victory? What rules can we set for our tactics at this point to ensure they support our strategy? Indeed, what can all the testosterone-fuelled philosophies of Sun Tzu offer us in today's environment, where charging around an office dressed as a sword-wielding Chinese warrior is unlikely to be seen as appropriate behaviour?

As ever, I searched the business and personal texts for the definitive answers. But then I jotted down my own and thought these as strong as anything I could find from reading all those business books:

* Tactics are nothing more than a series of moves aimed at meeting our objectives. Most often they are moves arranged in a linear form (i.e., one after the other).
* Tactics are mostly action points – contact this person, write this letter, make that phone call, get that meeting. But they can also be developmental – find out about that course, develop this skill.
* In fact, you should organize your tactics under a series of headings, such as research, skill acquisition, relationship building – or something more immediate such as applications, contacts, books to read, etc.
* Tactics can be tiny steps or giant leaps. Giant leaps are rare, however, and can often move you to the wrong place. In fact, where possible, giant leaps should be converted into a series of tiny steps that produce a series of small victories.
* Planned action points need to involve both the next steps and the second series of steps after the first milestones have been reached.
* Immediate tactics should focus on your strengths while medium-term tactics can look towards overcoming your weaknesses.
* Those looking at overcoming weaknesses should focus on gathering information or on acquiring skills for medium-term milestones.
* Execution tactics are only for where we have the strength to act. Bold leaps based purely on bravado are pointless, potentially wasteful and should be avoided.

- Don't execute tactics on too many fronts. Concentrate energies in one place in order to gain small victories. And then move on.
- Use your diary to determine deadlines, calculate priorities, assess your outcomes and record your (small) victories (and setbacks).
- Deadlines should be the key determinant of the order in which you tackle the action points, although make sure each action moves you towards your goal and that key deadlines are not being missed elsewhere that may be more important for your objectives (see also *Managing the Process* below).
- Work out the cost (in every respect – mental, financial, social, physical) of each tactic beforehand and be prepared to pay it. Baulking at the cost halfway through is the quickest way to derail an entire campaign.
- In fact, factor in some overspend – it is bound to happen.
- Don't start a tactic without a clear idea of its outcome, and focus purely on that outcome – most alternative outcomes will, in reality, be setbacks.
- But be flexible. Outcomes are unpredictable. We may have to change tactics quickly when outcomes do not go as planned. As the Prussian field marshal Helmuth von Molke said: "No plan survives contact with the enemy".
- Be aware of the potential downside of any tactic – and plan for it. But don't expect it. Expect to win a small victory.

What's Stopping You? *After goal-setting you need to develop a strategy – the bridge that ensures your tactical action points are focused on your objectives. Your strategy needs to take account of your strengths and weaknesses. Tactics, meanwhile, are the tiny steps you take daily – allowing small victories to build into significant progress.*

10

JUDGEMENT AND IDEAS

Good judgement is the key to executing any plan. We need the ability to make the right decisions at the right moments. Yet those with a high fear of failure struggle with respect to judgement. For instance, how many times are we told to make decisions relying on our gut instinct when, as High-FFs, our gut instinct may be derived from fear, insecurities and perceived slights and prejudices against us? For the recovering High-FF, gut instinct is something we may have to ignore or overcome in order to make strong decisions.

In *Judgement* (2007) leadership academics Noel M. Tichy and Warren G. Bennis state that solid judgement requires a good character and a strong internal "moral compass", both of which – as High-FFs – we may feel we lack. Yet strong long-term goals and a thought-through strategy offer us the most powerful possible benchmarks for our decisions – making any judgements not about us but about the pursuit of our goals. And if we divide our activities into objectives, strategies and tactics, we are capable of making decisions at a lower level that – no matter what the outcome – should have no immediate bearing at the higher level.

Judgement calls in three stages

According to Tichy and Bennis, judgement calls are made in three stages. There is the "pre" stage, discerning the actual judgement required and "framing and naming" the judgement needed. This is followed by the "call" in which the decision is made, although we first gather as much information as we need, which may lead to the realization that we do not have enough information or need to enlist different people. And finally there is the "execution", which is making our decision happen. This requires commitment.

And if this sounds like a recipe for protracted decision making, so be it. Strong decisions take time to get right, especially for the recovering High-FF with a past wrecked by poor decision making.

"Good judgement is not one terrific *aha* moment after another," write Tichy and Bennis. "In the real world, good judgement, at least on the big issues that make a difference, is usually an incremental process."

This chimes well with Stephen Covey (1989) who states that the best way to improve our responses is to focus on the distance "between stimulus and response". If we can lengthen this distance our decisions will be less focused on our emotions (a common High-FF trait) and more focused on achieving our goals, which should produce better results.

The joy of crises

Tichy and Bennis also state that decision making is in three domains: judgements about people, judgements about strategy, and judgements in times of crisis. We will deal with people below and have dealt with strategy above – so what about judgements in a crisis?

Crises are the moments for the recovering High-FF to step out of the shadows and step up to the plate – not least because the potential for humiliation has been removed. Failed is the current state, our worst-case scenario has arrived, allowing the High-FF to take humiliation-free risks – which takes us back to Gene Kranz and his "failure is not an option" moment.

Certainly, we must take responsibility for dealing with a crisis when it comes. Blame can wait for calmer moments, although we should thank those responsible for giving us the opportunity to make strong decisions from (usually) a depersonalized perspective. According to Steve Chandler (2001) we should look for the gift within every problem. For instance, in public relations the most regular crisis we face is an unhappy client. If the cause is external – some poor publicity perhaps – then the crisis will strengthen their dependence on us. We are the fire brigade arriving just in time to put out the flames and direct the clean up (usually involving a nice lunch with the offending journalist in order to "re-educate" them). If the crisis is internal – they are unhappy with us – then this is usually a good opportunity to go back to the Campaign Plan, reassess the tactics and (after repeated tactical failures) ensure we have the right strategy.

If the problem really is with *us* then it is often a chance for me to step in and show my team what I can do to soothe a client's anger. I can take charge of a project or return to the fore with respect to running the account, which will do my stock little harm with both my employees and the client. If even that fails and we lose the account – which is rare given the structural strength of our Campaign Plans – we then have a major opportunity to learn from our mistakes and perhaps reshuffle the team.

50:50s

A final point on judgement deals with those 50:50 choices – especially when it isn't always apparent which route best supports our long-term objectives. Deciding between closely aligned university places, career paths, job offers, promotions or even potential employees are key moments in our life and they can, for the High-FF, trigger fear-based insecurities that lead to false evaluations and major mistakes, or indecision at best. If life comes down to a handful of decisions, these are them – and they are usually the moments, above all else, that provide the monkey with resulting evidence he needs regarding our innate awfulness.

There is no easy way of dealing with such decisions, and no way of completely removing the fear. My own method has been to draw two columns headed by our choices – say UCL or UEA – with the rows the factors influencing the decision. For universities these would include such things as: structure of course, course reputation, college reputation, city, distance from home, other friends attending, nightlife and accommodation. We then need to score each and, importantly, weight each (perhaps banding a few of the peripherals – such as city and nightlife – together). And if it gives us the result we didn't want, then the exercise at least helps confirm the choice we favour.

And we should not regret the decision. Regret is a major trait of the High-FF, with us spending much of our lives pondering parallel universes; "if only" we'd made this or that choice. Of course, the rival world is always the one in which we have achieved our goals and lost our fears, leaving us cursing our poor decision making or hesitancy regarding opportunities. Meanwhile, our purgatory continues in the real world – with those regrets piling up just beyond every decision-requiring crossroads.

Yet regretting the unknown is madness. It is self-inflicted torture and a cheap victory for the monkey. And it is easily refuted, simply because we are – indeed – High-FFs. As stated, the insecurities that dog High-FFs are innate. There is no decision or outcome that will remove our fears, so the feelings we have now we'd still have – even if we'd made all the right decisions and achieved all our wildest dreams (as stated, an insight into celebrity behaviour is all the evidence required to prove this point).

And we must remember that each lifespan involves multiple 50:50 moments. Sheer probability tells us that we'll get some right and some wrong, so it is self-defeating to simply focus on those we potentially (but not certainly) got wrong.

Of course, as High-FFs such balanced thinking is a stretch, so we could always focus on the fact that, "knowing our luck", we'd have probably been run over by a bus on the first day along the alternative road.

The false hope of ideas

Like judgements, ideas are key execution tools. And, again, they are a problematic area for those handicapped with a high fear of failure. Many High-FFs are very good at generating ideas, although most of us fall at the first hurdle when it comes to implementation. Over time, this renders us incapable of differentiating between good and bad ideas, which – sadly – leaves us haunted by our creativity (especially when we see our ideas being implemented by others). For those with a high fear of failure ideas can seem like pipe-dreams, often giving us nothing more than false hope and an additional layer of frustration.

Other High-FFs, however, can struggle to think imaginatively – perhaps because, so trapped are they in their current status, they have switched off their creative brain. So while the sensitivity of the High-FF lends itself to creativity, poor experiences may mean we have extinguished the flame or – potentially worse – become tormented by our own ideas.

And this is bad news when trying to implement a strategy for meeting our objectives because navigating the "rocks in the river" (to quote Robbins) requires strong imagination as well as strong judgement.

According to advertising executive Jack Foster in *How to Get Ideas* (1996) people who come up with good ideas know they exist and know they will find them, which can, initially, seem unhelpful. What if we are not confident that good ideas exist? If Foster states that the most important factor needed for successful idea generation is self-belief, then those without it are surely doomed, at least in terms of idea generation.

But there is hope. For Foster, the key problem is being a grown up. Adults think too much. They are hampered by experience, which – for those with a high fear of failure – is usually negative experience. Boundaries, rules, fears: all crowd in on the adult trying to generate ideas.

So the answer is to be more like children. As children we all indulged in imaginative play without rules or boundaries, so we need – once again – to tap into that childlike freedom of illogical and silly creativity.

"Kids are natural born scientists," says Foster, quoting astronomer Carl Sagan. "First of all they ask the deep scientific questions. Why is the moon round? . . . By the time they get into High School they hardly ever ask questions like that."

For the High-FF, this is because the fear of failure has kicked in – with all the attendant concerns regarding public humiliation.

Yet nearly all children go through the "why" stage, and we should do our best to return to that wonderfully creative period when young eyes are looking and articulating thoughts and ideas for the first time.

In fact, this is highly possible for the High-FF. As stated, High-FFs are often sensitive types who have ideas but then fear the criticism that airing such ideas may bring. Yet this is no different to any creative: designers, writers, artists are all overly-sensitive to criticism. The difference between them and us (as High-FFs) is that they manage to overcome their fears. How? By pursuing strong objectives via well-thought-through strategies and well-executed tactics. This has meant that their RAS is tuned to their creativity, not to their sensitivity.

High-FFs, meanwhile, are tuned incorrectly, which either blocks creativity totally or paralyses any potential our creativity generates. With our RAS set to goal achievement, however, our ideas are likely to be more useful to our positive pursuits, rather than our darkest contemplations.

A technique for producing ideas

James Webb Young is the Sun Tzu of ideas. And in his 1960s book *A Technique for Producing Ideas* he set out what he saw as a strong process for advertising creatives to follow when trying to think up campaigns in that burgeoning industry.

"The production of ideas is just as definite a process as the production of Fords," was Webb Young's view.

He stated that there were general principles that underpinned the production of ideas, and that these included the notion that ideas are, more or less, "a new combination of old elements". This is not dissimilar to a comedian's thought process (Foster suggests we study comedians if we are struggling to think like children) and, like the comic, the key need is the ability to see relationships between different elements in order to create a new (perhaps funny) version of reality.

Webb Young followed this up with a simple and intuitive step-by-step methodology:

* Gather *all* the "raw materials" relating to your immediate problem – both general and specific.
* Store them in a way that allows for easy and quick reference (this means visually rather than electronically). He suggests writing notes on those classic 6 × 4 inch indexing cards or in a scrapbook.
* Mull over the information – play with it, read it again and again. Notice different – not necessarily relevant – aspects of the information.
* Incubate this information. Go and do something else (Webb Young cites Sherlock Holmes always taking the rational and irritated Watson to a concert halfway through a case).
* Come back to the information afresh and look for the "eureka" moment.
* Develop the idea into its final shape – perhaps asking others to evaluate it.

But what if this only throws up rotten ideas? According to Foster, there is no such thing as a bad idea. As with Thomas Edison and his experiments with lightbulbs/rubber, bad ideas are no more than part of the elimination process for the creation of good ideas. And some bad ideas are not bad ideas at all – they just haven't been judged correctly. For instance, Richard Drew – the inventor of Scotch tape (as Sellotape is known in the US) – was told to "take this tape . . . and shove it" by the person first trialing it.

No ideas are final

Yet we need to be aware that no ideas are final. For every good idea we have there is, according to Foster, an even better one out there. This should motivate us to supplement our ideas with refinements and additions but also to quickly replace our weaker ideas with new and stronger ones. In fact, as long as we are thinking of ideas, we are in the correct frame of mind for thinking up the right idea.

Foster's other tips for idea creation included:

* *Thinking visually* – people who think with pictures generate more ideas than people who think with words.
* *Thinking laterally* – goal achievement may be linear but, with ideas, one point should not follow the next. Great sideways leaps matter – as do leaps that seem to have no direction at all.
* *Don't assume boundaries* – ideas should not have assumed restrictions forced upon them, at least not at the idea-generation stage.
* *Set some limits* – although seemingly contradictory, some ideas can come from tighter definition. If we have to describe something in 900 words or design something within a particular space, then this restriction can be the spark for the imaginative leap. Foster points out that the invention of the Caesar salad, for instance, came about due to the chef having only those ingredients to work with.

> **What's Stopping You?** *Strong goal-setting and a thought-through strategy help you make better judgements that are free of typical High-FF insecurities. They also free your creativity, helping you produce strong ideas that can help your tactical progress.*

11

MANAGING THE PROCESS

"**M**anage the process" was a line delivered to me by my then future, now former, boss. At the bank's annual offsite he invited me, as a financial journalist, to give a speech on the competitive landscape of corporate banking.

Motivated to deliver my first-ever speech involving my specialist knowledge to a group of actual practitioners, I worked long and hard to get the presentation right and to deliver it perfectly. There was also the sniff of a job in the air.

On the day, I spent all morning in my hotel room practicing in front of the mirror and then did everything I could to mentally prepare myself, including going for a swim just prior to the speech to help me appear relaxed and authoritative. Boy was I prepared, although not for the midday lockout from my room with my notes either inside or in the cleaner's trash – all because I'd forgotten to request an extended check out.

In fact I'd ignored the warning from the organizers that this would happen – being too focused on the speech to take any notice of practical or pressing considerations.

"Manage the process, *laddie*," my future boss said as I tripped in to the lecture hall late and flustered from my desperate and overly-emotional exchanges with the cleaning supervisor. The notes had not been trashed, but had been "tidied", so I was terrified throughout that I'd be flummoxed by each new slide, meaning my delivery was nervous and poor.

My great speech had been ruined, not least by my future boss's patronising comment. In fact I quietly resented it. As comments go it was hardly aimed at easing my nerves. Yet this didn't stop me adopting the motto for my own team in future years. While its wisdom was obvious, it had that all-important edge of superiority about it that I enjoyed. It sounded like something a boss should say to a flustered subordinate – one over-burdened with the expectations of his or her superiors without any of their advantages (PAs, support systems, first-class tickets – years of experience).

But whatever its inadequacy as an encouragement to a team member, it's a useful mantra for us when trying to organize our lives for achievement motivation. This is about getting the small stuff right. About organizing ourselves in such a way that allows time and space for the execution of our strategy and tactics. This is the bit where we overcome mental hurdles such as "I just haven't the time" or "I'm too busy" or "I'm just too disorganized".

Anyone can adopt efficient practices

So what's meant by "managing the process"? To my former/future boss it meant no more than "work out what has to be done, when, and do it". And there may be little need to add more to the definition, except to offer the view that time-and-task management is not a skill, or a talent, or even a craft. It is, indeed, a process. There is nothing innate about efficiency. Anyone can adopt efficient practices – we just have to set ourselves up to be efficient, follow that through, and then turn that process into a habit.

Just as the modern kitchen is organized to allow meal preparation in minutes – if so desired – and just as the modern bathroom allows for quick-turnaround ablutions in the morning, so we can organize other aspects of our lives to create the same levels of efficiency, as long as we set ourselves up correctly and then follow through.

"Getting control of your time means facing up to the fact that you are usually the problem, not someone else," says time-management guru Alec MacKenzie in *The Time Trap* (1972), the mother of all time-management books. "It means doing the hard work of changing well-established habits. It means holding your ground against the negative tugs of human nature."

MacKenzie talks of human characteristics that contradict the laws of time management – such as ego, the desire to please, the fear of offending and the fear of new challenges – all of which are well known to those with a high fear of failure. We may think controlling our work environment is beyond us. Yet giving in to outside pressures is something that resides within *us*, says MacKenzie – using the example of answering the phone when we are busy and then blaming the caller for the interruption.

Covey's four activity boxes

So can we clear the clutter from our path towards progress? Absolutely, although we must first clear the clutter from our thinking.

According to Stephen Covey (1989) every activity in our waking hours belongs in one of four boxes (or "quadrants") in what he calls the "time management matrix". This important-sounding concept simply suggests that all activities are either "urgent" or "not urgent" and – additionally – that all activities are either "important" or "not important".

In my (slightly altered) version the boxes are labelled:

- *Box 1* – urgent and important
- *Box 2* – urgent and not important
- *Box 3* – not urgent and important
- *Box 4* – not urgent and not important.

Covey contends that we spend most of our time on activities in one of the two "urgent" boxes – marked either "important" or "not important". And while Box 1 may contain valuable work such as immediate but worthwhile tasks and goal-oriented projects with tight deadlines, we will always turn to Box 2 as soon as they are done – simply because tasks in Box 2 are also "urgent" and therefore shout louder.

Yet this is a disaster for our progress. Box 2, of urgent but unimportant tasks, is the box that knocks the High-FF off course. Unable to prioritize, fearful of saying no, we try and balance Boxes 1 and 2 but have only the vaguest notion of what activities are important for goal achievement and what requires our focus simply to get someone off our back. And the two combined wipe out our potential for growth, which is nearly all stored in Box 3 – containing not urgent but nonetheless important tasks.

Box 2 deceives us into thinking we are making progress, but is in fact no more than the processing of interruptions such as emails, phone calls, meetings, enquiries from adjacent colleagues and other ultimately useless activities. Box 3, meanwhile, contains important future-oriented activities such as research, relationship-building, applications, skill-acquisition and planning.

Amazingly, Box 3 is the least loved of all the boxes, despite being the most important. Exhausted after a day working through Boxes 1 and 2, we flop into the escapist "not urgent, not important" activities of Box 4. This really is the time-wasters' box – usually involving mind-numbing TV or Internet surfing – although can include some pleasant activities that could potentially be recategorized as "important", such as family time or exercise, once we are on top of time-and-task management.

Rethinking the notion of time

So how can we create the space to focus on Box 3? A key requirement is to rethink our notion of time.

"We may have leisure time, but no one has such a thing as free time," says corporate consultant and academic B. Eugene Griessman in *Time Tactics of Very Successful People* (1994). "You may be lying by the pool or attending a play, but that's not free time. All time has value."

Griessman states that you should develop a full appreciation of the value of time, if necessary allocating a theoretical monetary cost for each hour depending on what you think an hour of your time is worth. Although mentally doubling your current hourly rate is a good starting point, the aim is not to be "crudely materialistic". It is to help you realize that – if you are in a meeting that's dragging on, or you are talking too frequently to your colleague – you understand the true cost *to you* of that meeting or conversation (or even that wasteful out-of-hours activity).

If necessary, says Griessman, you should keep a log of your daily ration of 24 hours (perhaps in your diary) so that you can analyze over a period where you have allocated your time, and its cost. Quickly it should become apparent where the efficiencies are to be had – what activities are in the unimportant boxes and should, therefore, be squeezed or eliminated.

Create a timetable

Yet Griessman's recommendations can seem complicated. Covey's simpler approach, meanwhile, takes us back to school – actually creating a school-style timetable with hourly slots from eight-til-eight and blocks for the evening. You should allocate each hour of the day for particular activities – importantly, allowing you to schedule time for the vital Box 3 activities that help you make progress towards your goals.

The timetable uses all seven days and requires you to state your weekly and daily priorities and your weekly goals against your particular roles (e.g. father, husband, manager, future entrepreneur). And while you need to be realistic about time allocation for each task, you also need to be strict on yourself regarding the need to complete tasks within the allotted timeframe before moving on – not engaging in other activities until you have completed your tasks.

Yet even this can become unsustainable. Such an approach will work well for initially improving your time-management practices – as well as making you acutely aware of being bamboozled by Box 2 activities. But only the most swivel-eyed self-motivators will want to regiment their lives to the point where the kids are being dragged to badminton because that's what it says on the timetable. It is also an easy timetable to write but one less easy to follow because your energy and motivation levels are not always consistent. Slotting in two hours last thing on Friday afternoon for "ideas and creativity" may be pushing your luck with respect to motivation, for instance, although it may be just the time to discuss ideas in the pub with the rest of the team.

In *The Time Trap* MacKenzie suggests you understand your personal energy cycle before setting up your "ideal day" with respect to timetabling. And, certainly, you need some flexibility within the system, although what I notice when strictly pursuing Covey's timetable is that if I follow it from Monday, such strong time-structuring means most of my Box 1 and 2 tasks are complete by Wednesday, allowing me to focus on Box 3 items for Thursday and Friday (and on reframed Box 4 activities at the weekend).

Proactively managing interruptions

But what of those nasty Box 2 items, derailing our agendas? Of course, it's impossible to kill all interruptions – at least without making ourselves unpopular. Yet it may help to allot particular times for dealing with them – perhaps from 9am to10am and/or from 5pm to 6pm. It just might be the case that you can also politely and over time train those around you to respect those hours for "urgent" but not important interruptions.

Well, you can at least try, although it may be helped by proactivity on your part – Box 2 interruptions are usually from a handful of the same individuals, so a quick call at 9am – asking if they have all they need for the day because "I need to knuckle down on a major project and will be keen to minimize interruptions" – may just work if delivered in a style aimed at making their work seem valued and necessary (rather than the eye-rolling job-creation you may inwardly believe it to be).

Clearing roadblocks

Yet what if you can't even get this far – so cluttered is the path in front of you? This usually means there's a roadblock preventing you getting started. A roadblock so large, what's more, that you cannot see the road ahead because of it. In *Getting Things Done* (2001), executive coach David Allen accepts that your first job may be to create the sense of control and focus you need for the journey – perhaps clearing that major project or task by writing a list of everything you need to do to move that project forward.

This may be a struggle, although as long as you remain clear about the intention of making headway towards your goals, you should soon manage to navigate the obstacle. And even with the roadblock, Covey's timetable may help breathe some oxygen into your schedule – perhaps allowing an hour a day on Box 3 activities – even while in the thick of the fight to overcome your roadblock.

In *The Power of an Hour* (2006), "business acceleration" consultant Dave Lakhani discusses the "critical power hour" that allows you to address such major roadblocks by working out what you need to change, what is the structure of the change, what solutions are possible, what are the next steps, and how you will reward yourself once done. As the name of his book suggests, Lakhani divides life's tasks into hours that have a "fearsome focus" with a relaxing break at the end.

"While time may seem like the thing you need the most of," he says, "it turns out that isn't true. What you need is focus – a very specific kind of focus."

This complements Covey's timetable. And Lakhani's recommendations also chime with David Allen's advice that, when facing that initial roadblock, you first create a physical place that captures everything you need to get done – now, later or some time – into a logical and organized system, such as a ring-binder. Just maybe your roadblock is not as large as it seems, once you have properly assessed its proportions and how it might be navigated.

"Sharpening the saw"

One of my favourite tricks for unblocking "big-taskitis" is to buy some stationery. These are the tools of the organized person and, just as a mountaineer will spend hours looking at equipment for an expedition – seeing it as a thrilling precursor to the adventure ahead – so you should fall in love with the stationery store. Files, folders, wallets, organizers, in-trays, memo-pads: this is the equipment you need to climb your mountain and you should indulge yourself with new and shiny objects and arrange them lovingly around your desk.

You should also spend time arranging your desk. David Allen states that you should schedule a block of time dedicated to preparing your workstation: sourcing the necessary furniture, cabinets, in-trays and electronic equipment, making sure it is arranged as you want it, is configured and primed to your needs, and is both efficient and pleasing to look at. Once done, you should admire it. It will be your cockpit for the journey ahead.

This is what Stephen Covey calls "sharpening the saw" – his seventh habit, in fact. In *Seven Habits . . .* he offers a parable in which a man, struggling to fell a tree is advised to sharpen the old rusty saw he is using.

"I don't have time to sharpen the saw, I'm too busy sawing," says the man, and struggles on inefficiently.

Just about every "success" writer agrees with this, even Abraham Lincoln.

"Give me six hours to chop down a tree and I will spend the first four sharpening the axe," is one of his attributed quotes.

Certainly, preparation is a key part of our drive for time-and-task efficiency, as are the right tools.

"Make your workplace work for you," says Griessman (1994), adding that you should spend money on the files and equipment you need to work efficiently and affectively.

And if memo-pads and files sound a bit "last century", so they should. Sure Covey's timetable can be electronic, as can project documents. However, Allen's idea of a "collection bucket" for anything unfinished, so it can be "released from your mind" but still apparent as a "to do", needs to be physical in my view. My PC's hard-drive is full of electronic folders that have been created and then forgotten, yet every physical file that has ever been on my desk has been dealt with, no matter how far down the pile it sank or even if it was eventually consciously thrown away. The key thing is that it wasn't lost and forgotten.

"To do" lists and "checklists"

This is also true of reminders or "to do" lists. These can even be in your diary, although I'd rather not have my diary so visible – preferring instead those 6 × 4-inch lined cards where I list my tasks for the next few days, crossing them off when complete. The size of the card is important as I can only fit 12 or so tasks on the list before having to start a new card. Sure, some tasks get relegated, and some cards need to have undone tasks transferred between them. Yet the simple process of transferring a task from one card to another reminds me of the task and helps me reassess it. The cards are then propped behind my keyboard and stare at me all day. Box 2 interruptions are simply given a line on the card and dealt with between 5pm and 6pm.

Importantly, Box 3 needs are given equal billing to Box 1. And any "manage the process" elements, such as a need to renew my passport, collect my suit from the dry cleaners or buy my wife's birthday present(s) also get a line, as well as a line through them once done.

"Learn to rely on checklists," recommends Griessman (1994), although he also states that these are not to be confused with "to do" lists (as described above). Checklists note the steps we must take to complete a task efficiently. For instance, everything we need for a trip abroad is a checklist, everything I needed to do to allow me to focus on nothing but my speech – including quick calls to reception to request a late checkout – is a checklist.

Checklists are about capturing everything, although order is also important. In *Getting Things Done*, David Allen states that there are five stages when dealing with workflow:

- *Collect* – create a (physical) file to capture everything that is on your to-do list.
- *Process* – work out how to deal with each item. Is it for now or after another item? What needs doing? Is it perhaps for "reference only" or "research further" or "contact now"?
- *Organize* – create a system (perhaps a checklist) that reflects your decisions regarding priority and the actionable plans you have for each item.
- *Do* – undertake the actionables. Allen recommends one of four criteria for making sure you are in the best place for action. Context (which location – home, work?), time (how long do you need and have you timetabled that block?), energy (can you see this through to completion?), and priority (is this the "now" task, or is there something else more pressing – though beware the Box 2 bully? If not now, when?).

- *Review* – use Covey's timetable to slot weekly review moments for the file – going back to "process".

Griessman would perhaps add "get it done now" to Allen's list. He states that it is damaging to start a project, put it away, and then start again – spending time wondering "where was I?". Some projects cannot be finished in one go but many can and should. Also, you should stop midway only after giving yourself clear written instructions about what comes next once you restart.

Griessman also suggests that you "ask yourself, 'is there an easier way to do this?'"

"Looking for the easy way out can be the smartest thing you can do," he says. "Don't confuse 'busyness' with efficiency."

Deal with the worst thing first

A final Griessman tip worth adopting is to deal with unpleasant situations first. Immediately tackling the tasks that give us least comfort can make them more bearable. Indeed, these tasks are often the very roadblocks that are obscuring the way ahead.

Brian Tracy (of *Goals!* fame) writes something similar in *Eat That Frog* (2004), although uses more descriptive language – suggesting that if you "eat a live frog each morning" you will have already experienced the worst thing that will happen to you that day. He says you should find the live frogs that are hidden on your to-do list or checklists and tackle them first – learning to "snack on those difficult problems".

Of course by frogs Tracy means the largest and/or most important and/or most difficult task facing you on your path towards progress.

"The ability to concentrate single-mindedly on your most important task, to do it well and to finish it completely, is the key to great success," says Tracy – suggesting that the frogs are a "high-protein diet" that will give you the right physique for dealing with all the other tasks.

Prioritization and efficiency

This feeds into Tracy's thinking on prioritization – offering a tip that can easily be added to your to-do list or checklist or to Covey's timetable. He calls it the "ABCs of Success" although also adds D and E. His suggestion is that you categorize your to-do list with an ABCD or E. An "A" task is one that you must complete as soon as possible or "face serious consequences". "B" items are important tasks that carry "mild consequences". "C" tasks are nice to do but with "no consequences", "D" tasks can be delegated (see Part Four) and "E" tasks should be eliminated. Of course, the stressed person may be tempted to load their tasks with "A" and "B" labels, which Tracy says is fine – "simply number them sequentially . . . A-1, A-2, A-3 and so forth".

I also think it important to be opportunistic when it comes to efficiency. My to-do list is as much in my head as on my 6× 4 cards and I often send myself text messages on the rare occasions I have no pen and paper handy (which would earn me a "tut-tut" from entrepreneurs such as Richard Branson and Luke Johnson who are never without a small notepad and pen). This means that (helped by my RAS) I am always on the lookout for a chance to quickly fulfil a need. Queueless cashpoints always attract my eye, for instance, and I never pass the stationery store without it occurring to me that this may be a good moment to stock up.

Yet this can go beyond small tasks. Grabbing a coffee or a sandwich is a great opportunity to discuss a major project with a colleague; travel to meetings offers a strong chance to read boring documents that have to be digested (often called "airplane reading" in the US) or practice presentational skills with a colleague; and commuting offers us an excellent opportunity to undertake Box 3 tasks such as acquiring knowledge and research.

Endeavour is the key

Does all this sound a bit manic? Perhaps it should. In his ground-breaking book *Outliers* (2008), renowned business author Malcolm Gladwell focuses on what turns ordinary mortals into outstanding achievers. One clear trait is endeavour. In tracking potential professional musicians, he states that researchers noticed a pattern between the hours of practice and the level of achievement. Strong amateurs put in around 2000 hours by adulthood while teachers put in around 4000. Professionals, however, put in around 8000 hours and the elite 10,000.

"Virtually every success story . . . involves someone or some group working harder than their peers," was Gladwell's conclusion.

Hard work matters. No-one else will achieve your goals on your behalf. But does that mean you are never off duty, never relaxed? All this activity can make you feel and appear hyper, which can irritate those around you and lead to nervous exhaustion. Your aim here is not to alienate people who may now seem to you disinterested, disorganized and, frankly, in the slow lane. You are simply trying to make progress towards *your* goals by producing better results. You must realize that this may take time and may not always involve smooth progress, so you may need to inject some wind-down time within your schedule if you are not to burn out. And you must also realize that you remain connected to others – especially significant others – and shouldn't alienate them through your potentially over-zealous words and actions.

This means you should reframe those Box 4 "not urgent and not important" tasks. If they are the moments you reconnect with friends and family – making sure you are carrying them with you on your journey – then Box 4 has its place. If Box 4 tasks are also the moments you can recharge your batteries with exercise, disconnected stimulation or relaxation then they definitely have their place. And if they are, crucially, the moments you reflect on the tiny self-confirming steps you are taking each day then they are valuable indeed.

What's Stopping You? *Efficiency is not a skill or craft, it is a process anyone can adopt. You need to organize all your activities, scheduling your time correctly and setting yourself up for effective execution. Roadblocks, interruptions and time-wasting can all be dealt with to prevent them from halting your progress.*

PART FOUR
People

12

SELF-ESTEEM

We can develop strategies and execute tactics all we like. Sooner or later we are going to have to tackle people – probably the most challenging aspect of any recovery programme for those with high fear of failure.

"Fully 85 percent of your success in life is going to be determined by your social skills," says Brian Tracy in *Maximum Achievement* (1993), "by your ability to interact positively and effectively with others and to get them to cooperate with you in helping you to achieve your goals."

Tricky stats aside, this is by far the most difficult chapter for me to write. Over the years my High-FF behaviour has destroyed more business and office relationships, more friendships and more romantic involvements than I dare to remember. I have been truly dreadful when it comes to my dealings with my fellow human beings: hurtful, angry, destructive and self-centred. And that's just with the people who were on my side. Out of fear, I suspect I have behaved rather better to those who did not have my best interests at heart.

Throughout my life it has been me that has nursed the burning sense of injustice. I have sometimes treated people appallingly because of an overly-sensitized perception of prejudice against me, even from friends. I have jumped to every wrong conclusion, assumed every slight intended, absorbed every insult – meant or otherwise. I have also reacted angrily in defence on so many occasions that I have problems recalling any past period without immediately remembering some reactive episode I wish I could forget.

Yet High-FF reactivity goes way beyond angry responses. Poor reactions to social or people situations can equally encompass hurt, withdrawal and passivity, in which we fail to stand up for ourselves, or bitchiness and criticism, in which we seek revenge for perceived slights through backstabbing or passive aggressive behaviour such as being obstructive.

People skills are vital

Indeed, of all the failings of those with a high fear of failure, it is our dealings with people that most disable us. Another one of Tracy's stats (this one backed up by surveys) states that over 95 percent of men and women "let go" from their jobs in America over a 10-year period were fired because of poor social skills rather than lack of competence.

No matter how well you strategize to meet your objectives, if you fail to improve your people skills you will fail to make progress in your life. We cannot avoid people in the pursuit of our goals. In many respects, people *are* the goal as well as the means of achieving them. Yet they are also our greatest barrier. Without people skills we are illiterate in a land of words, innumerate in a land of numbers. We are deaf in a room filled with sound.

Those neural hijackings that act as the internal assassins of our objectivity are almost always triggered by someone else's words or actions, and our interpretations of the intentions behind them. Yet when dealing with people the depersonalisation we should employ to help overcome such hijackings seems impossible. If somebody insults me – perceived or otherwise – it's not *Me Inc.* that's being insulted. It's me.

Low self-esteem – the distorting mirror

As a recovering High-FF, however, it is important to recognize that much of the alienation we have felt has not only been conceived and perceived in our own heads, it has been self-fulfilling and therefore self-inflicted. Sure hateful people exist (though they are mostly fellow High-FFs). But the person who really hates you – to the core of your being – who really doesn't have your best interests at heart, is you.

This is an awful and depressing realization. Yet – like taking responsibility – it is also a liberating thought. If you are your own worst enemy then you are the person who can exorcise the demon within that is destroying not only your life chances, but your friendships, relationships, partnerships and leaderships. That demon has got to go – and you are the only person who can throw it out.

The key issue here – the distorting mirror that generates the problems – is low self-esteem. As stated in Part One, not all High-FFs suffer from low self-esteem, although most do to either a lesser or greater extent (usually greater) and there is a direct relationship between self-esteem and our ability to get along with others.

"The more you like and respect yourself," says Tracy, "the more you like and respect others. The more you consider yourself to be a valuable and worthwhile person, the more you consider others to be valuable and worthwhile as well. The more you accept yourself just as you are, the more you accept others just as they are."

And clearly this has a direct impact upon our ability to utilize the power of people to achieve our goals.

"Men and women with low self-esteem can only get along with a few people, and then not for very long," says Tracy. "Their low self-regard manifests itself in anger, impatience, criticism, bad-mouthing and arguments with the people around them."

As someone with low self-esteem this strikes home with painful clarity. We assume people do not like us because we dislike ourselves. This leads us to not like others, making their return of the feeling inevitable. Once again, we are in a self-fulfilling vortex with the dizzying addition that, according to Tracy, this is the single most important reason why so many people fail to meet their objectives.

Deconstructing low self-esteem

In *Boost Your Self-Esteem* (2003), John Caunt states that self-esteem issues present themselves in different ways, just about all of which are familiar to me. These include (with a few added thoughts of my own):

- Resenting others' success
- Feeling like a failure
- Focusing on the negative in any situation
- Allowing even "constructive" criticism to derail us
- Doing things purely to be liked or for approval
- Comparing ourselves continually and to our own detriment with others
- Taking *everything* too personally
- Giving in to others' desires
- Changing or arresting behaviour for fear of looking foolish
- Striving for perfection and being angry at not meeting unrealistic expectations
- Worrying excessively, but avoiding seeking help
- Feeling out of control, even panicking
- Bullying and taking advantage of others
- Putting ourselves and others down – publicly
- Withdrawing from or avoiding social situations
- Becoming aggressive, or even overly passive
- Being boastful
- Indulging in exaggeration if not downright lying in order to make ourselves more "interesting".

The persistence of such feelings – despite my strong growth thanks to the likes of Covey and Robbins *et al* – landed me back in the shrink's chair a year or so after my NHS counselling, determined to rid myself of the plagues of paranoia, fear, anger and low self-esteem that have conspired to make my entire life seem like a string of wrecked personal encounters.

Such appalling and disabling traits are, of course, developed from negative experiences in childhood. I was aware of what caused my own self-esteem issues, although further sessions with the psychoanalyst surprised me with respect to how they manifested themselves in my relationships. As a child, I knew I had a poor relationship with my father but hadn't realized I had subconsciously blamed my mother for this and therefore developed a resentment and irritation with the very person that had loved me the most. I also feared and resented the power of my sister – the apple of my father's eye.

Even writing this is painful but there it is: fear of rejection from the people whose love I sought while rejecting those who loved me unconditionally. Meanwhile, with peers: distrust, frustration, envy, paranoia. I didn't stand a chance of being able to develop strong social or people skills – I was far too busy throwing affection at those who didn't deserve it while collecting and then rejecting the commitment of those that did. As for peers, how could I be a suitable colleague or partner when, through mistrust and jealousy, I misinterpreted their every move?

As stated, self-esteem issues can have a profound impact on our ability to make progress in the workplace. We may be stymied by our inner beliefs and perceptions to the point where we develop coping mechanisms to avoid pain, such as rejecting ourselves before others are allowed to. Perhaps we don't put ourselves forward for promotion – convincing ourselves it would be the wrong move. Or we adopt the persona of the office clown or the unthreatening (perhaps even withdrawn) "nice guy" that's happier among the troops than the officers. And we avoid confrontation because we cannot trust either our internal or external responses.

At least, those are the better responses. We could become the brooding back-stabber, the angry shouter (that was me) or the scheming Machiavellian. All are the typical traits of those with low self-esteem. And all are a disaster.

The fight back

So is there anything we can do? Of course. We can fight back, although we must remember the battle is internal. We have already spent our lives externalising the battle with respect to dealing with people (even if just through withdrawal or submission). Now we must internalize it – turning the fire on the enemy within.

As I have stated before, there is no magic formula that can cure us, of either high fear of failure or low self-esteem. Our insecurities are not going to be wished (or self-hypnotized or acupunctured) away. Our default position is to undermine our self-belief and so encourage failure. Yet we can take small and progressive steps that help us develop better external responses, especially when it comes to dealing with people. We have been incorrectly wired to give a false reading on the intentions of others so that we interpret their actions wrongly and react inappropriately: defensiveness and anger at one end, shyness and withdrawal at the other – with us potentially flipping between these extremes.

Yet we must always remember that we are probably wrong. Did that person insult me, or dismiss me, or blank me? Maybe, but why assume so? If we assume it probably came out badly and they meant something more supportive or were distracted (as in the CBT example mentioned in Part One) then the result will almost certainly be better than if we assume the insult. This assumption may not be your first response, but can you make it your second? And can you make it your second response quickly – so quickly that you manage to externally suppress your first response? In time, hopefully, yes.

Judged by intentions, not actions

Like most people, I want to be judged on my intentions, not my actions, which may be misinterpreted for any number of reasons. So how can I deny this right to others? We must seek their intentions, not judge their actions.

If someone is brandishing a knife or gun in front of us it may be right to assume their intentions are aggressive. But there are thankfully few situations where this happens. And unlike guns or knives, words and body-language are open to wild misinterpretation. By assuming a better, kinder, interpretation – however hard this is to achieve – we are making it easier to respond appropriately.

In fact, the harder it is to perceive a kinder interpretation the more it is in your advantage to seek and assume one. Let's go back to the man brandishing the knife or gun. This is a pretty clear act of aggression, most would agree. Yet look behind the weapon at the man and he may perceive *us* as the aggressor. He may be protecting a child or be expecting an attack from someone else, or he may have snapped at the series of negative events that led him to this awful point. He may even be drug-addled and therefore not in control of his perceptions or responses. So, while we need to deal with the threat, looking behind it may also generate a more disarming response from us.

See the best in others

Seeing the best in people is incredibly difficult. Yet it is absolutely in your advantage to do so. If the gunman's actions are hostile you are going to take the bullet no matter what. But if they are defensive then your hostility is going to escalate the situation to the point when he feels so threatened he'll shoot in apparent self-defence.

Yet what if we are totally wrong and our harshest interpretation is correct?

So what? By forcing ourselves to assume a kinder interpretation of their intentions – we misheard, they didn't realize what they were saying, they are very stressed, we have given them the wrong signals and made them defensive – we are neutralizing the impact their insult/slight will have on us. In fact, as with Eleanor Roosevelt's famous quote – "No one can make you feel inferior without your consent" – we are saying it has no impact. This throws the insult back to them. They have thrown a bomb but it didn't go off – *how embarrassing!*

This is absolutely on-the-money when it comes to my issues with anger. Countless times I have overreacted to a perceived insult and the fallout from the insult has been about *my* response rather than *their* insult – all adding to my burning sense of injustice. But I have learned that – painful is this may seem – assuming a kinder intention on their part is the *only* way of developing a better response from me.

Spreading positivity

And assuming a kinder intention (however forced it feels at first) has further benefits. It starts to undermine the other props of your low self-esteem. By developing positivity about something – anything – it can spread elsewhere, even to you. In *Boost Your Self-Esteem* John Caunt suggests we practise techniques that reframe the information we feed our brain, helping create more positive attitudes and opinions. Over time and with positive and reinforcing steps, these help build our self-esteem, or at least disrupt the thought process that leads to our default low self-esteem assumptions.

These include (again, with some thoughts of my own):

• *Recognize your positive qualities.* This is one for the diary – listing all your good qualities. These are the qualities to focus on, not those you perceive as negative.

- *Indulge in positive self-talk.* Pay attention to what you say to yourself. Instead of self-harming language you must use positive or forgiving language. That monkey has no monopoly on your inner thoughts – he or she can and should be countered.
- *Question your thoughts and opinions.* Not just your views on others. You need to challenge your views on yourself – they are likely to be irrational and probably wrong. As Anthony Robbins says, there is no such thing as truth – only perception.
- *Associate with positive people.* Low-self-esteemers can find themselves in a negative club, especially in the office. Perhaps it is the smokers' coterie or the moaning canteen gang. Pull away from them, or – even better – start using positive language when with them (although avoid becoming the preaching motivational convert – remember, it is only *your* behaviour you are trying to change).
- *Acknowledge achievements.* You should keep a list (in the obvious place) of what you have achieved – however small. These are the building blocks of future achievement.
- *Accept what you cannot change.* Learn to accept what you cannot change (as with Covey's Circle of Concern). This may be more than just the weather but there is little about your situation that you cannot change with good planning and strong endeavour. Yet you need to be realistic and embrace the unchangeable, and that includes the past.
- *Detach yourself.* Yoga, sports, fiction, biographies – you must find something positive that takes you somewhere else, avoiding quick-fix diversions such as alcohol or drugs that will simply compound your negative feelings once they wear off.
- *Develop self-reliance.* You should not seek constant approval. Instead, you should trust your skills and be pleased with yourself without external affirmation. Don't seek to impress others – just be inwardly content with the small steps you are taking in the right direction.

- *Stop comparing yourself to others.* You are being unfair to yourself – we are all unique. You should not ape others but develop your singular qualities, although some mild NLP-style modelling of effective behaviour in others may help undermine your destructive behaviours (such as defensiveness in conversation). But don't *ever* wish to be someone else, not least because it is impossible, so such a desire will simply add to your frustration.

- *Learn to laugh at yourself.* You should laugh at your flaws – we all have them.

- *Accept praise.* Be graceful, but don't deflect it. You deserve it, though should not seek to expand it or reinforce it yourself. Just say "thank you".

- *Focus on the lessons.* From both your successes and your failures, there are lessons to be learned. You should seek them out and focus on those when you recall past errors, or even current successes.

- *Learn to say "no".* You should not be a people pleaser, just because you seek their approval. Your every action should be judged against your long-term goals and thought-through strategy, although keeping people onside will always be useful when pursuing your objectives.

Of course, the above points are easily written. Turning our self-harming and deeply-held assumptions into positives can feel like an impossible task, especially with that monkey offering negative feedback. Yet it is worth the effort and, in fact, can provide quick confirmation that we are heading in the right direction. Simply by reversing the direction we are travelling, we are immediately making headway towards our goals. And by noting that every small step leads to the next step – that every brick laid is the platform for the next brick – we can slowly, over time, get beyond the highest barrier of all: our own negative self view.

What's Stopping You? *"No one can make you feel inferior without your consent", so you should focus on reframing the thoughts and traits that undermine your self-esteem. Thinking more positively of those around you is an important building block for improving your own self view.*

13

DEALING WITH THE BOSS

Developing people skills is vital whether you are dealing with your boss, your peers and colleagues, your potential customers, or your employees. As a High-FF trying to make progress in your career, however, the person most likely to loom largest is your boss.

There's no getting away from it – working for a bad boss is hell. A bad boss can obsess, oppress and depress us – reducing a potentially-enjoyable job to a confidence-sapping imprisonment. Many people alter course in their careers, often with disastrous results, simply to escape a bad boss. My decision to become an entrepreneur, for instance, was majorly influenced by some appalling experiences in this respect (made far worse, no doubt, by the distorting mirror of my own insecurities).

Yet if you are convinced a key barrier for your progress is your current line manager you are far from alone. According to one study – quoted in *Dealing with the Boss from Hell* (2005) by leadership consultant Shaun Belding – around 75 percent of 1800 Australian workers surveyed stated they were unhappy with their managers, and US studies have produced similar findings.

And the reality, according to Belding, is that you have few remedies. Any direct confrontation is unlikely to produce positive results and could end up a "career limiting move" – jeopardizing rather than enhancing your progress.

"The hardest part of having a boss from hell is that very few resources are available to you for dealing with him or her," says Belding, so "don't shoot yourself in the foot" by publicly embarrassing, threatening or openly challenging your boss, he cautions.

Belding recommends that you wait before you act, you control your impulses and that you look beyond the immediate future towards the long-term consequences of your actions. Yet you can also develop some strong strategies and tactics aimed at not allowing a bad boss to derail your career.

Three types of bad boss

Belding states that bad bosses usually fall into one of three types – aggressive, passive or controlling – all of which throw up significant problems for less confident people. Yet, believe it or not, all also provide opportunities for progress. The aggressive boss can seem the most immediately debilitating. However, in most modern companies bullying behaviour such as shouting or intimidation is now viewed as unacceptable. So – while such behaviour is upsetting and potentially terrifying – the aggressive boss is, in my view, laying the foundations of his or her own demise.

Aggressive bosses are usually weak – often High-FFs themselves – and are therefore reasonably easy to manage once you realize this. Their behaviour is also usually well known, meaning that your suffering has probably been noticed by people further up the organization, although they may choose not to act. Deal well with the aggressive boss, and you will have acquired some significant and transferable people skills that will put you in a strong position no matter what your future.

Passive bosses also present opportunities. According to Belding, such bosses are usually shy and avoid decisions, conflicts, risks and strong individuals. They may be frustrating and inspire only contempt but they are also less likely to present a major barrier to your progress. In fact, in my opinion they are worth befriending and aiding. If you support their seniority, rather than undermine it, you are likely to have recruited perhaps your most significant ally towards your own goal achievement. Again, their weakness is unlikely to have gone unnoticed by their own reports, meaning that your assistance and support will also be noticed, although, again, this may not be obvious.

The Pisstaker's Charter

This brings me to the most difficult of all boss-related situations – dealing with someone trying to control or manipulate you, perhaps (in fact probably) leveraging off your insecurities in an attempt to steer the situation to their advantage. While aggressive or insulting bosses are often fellow High-FFs and therefore reasonably transparent in their aims, the manipulators have achievement motivation coursing through their veins and are far more difficult to read. They have also noticed your insecurities and are taking advantage.

I call this the *Pisstaker's Charter*: the notion that confident people can so effectively take advantage of under-confident people that we end up doing their bidding for them – with them even feigning surprise and hurt when we finally snap and resist. In fact, their surprise can be genuine, so used are they to getting the better of us by manipulating our insecurities, and so poor have we been at projecting our own needs.

My own experience here is a painful one – in fact, probably the most painful of my working life. The details need to remain obscure but such was the manipulation I experienced from one line manager that I felt was taking advantage of my low confidence that I was forced to fight back. Certainly I felt I was being used in ways that compromised my position, first as a screen for what I saw as his unethical behaviour and later as the person I felt was being blamed for its consequences.

Eventually, my career became so threatened by his actions that I had to report him. News came to me that the senior management were contemplating firing *me* with respect to *my* conduct (as reported by him) despite the fact it was, in my view, clearly *his* behaviour causing the problems. Given this, I felt I had no choice but to act. I spoke of my suspicions to the senior management and, within a few (agonising) months, he was gone.

Developing better responses

My actions resulted in someone losing their job and I have lived with the guilt ever since. And if that sounds odd given the circumstances, I see it as a sign of my growth that I can now see that it was my poor handling of the episode that allowed it to escalate. And it was my insecurities that caused it to develop in the first place. The situation was my fault, not his.

Here's what I could have done differently:

- *I could have been less emotional.* My overly-emotional responses when the problems developed weakened my position – especially with the senior management – and lost me the respect of colleagues and allies. Of course, it is difficult for insecure people to simply switch off their emotions – especially when we feel an injustice is being perpetrated – but it is possible. Taking time to rationalize the situation, perhaps by writing notes, would have been one way. Another would have been through knowing *all* the facts.
- *I could have been on top of the details.* Indeed, the key issues came down to facts and figures, so there was no need for my overly-emotional responses when a forensic look at the details would have provided the answers. I should have been like Lieutenant Columbo after a murder, sifting through the evidence line by line. I could have calmly kept on asking questions, and – if blocked – I could have suggested a third party gets involved, perhaps one of the senior managers. In truth, I had a very poor handle on the details, and it was this as much as

my insecurities that gave him room for manoeuvre. In fact, some of the more minor problems *were* my fault, which gave me an inner sense of guilt and him all the space he needed to make hay. In any manipulative situation, the facts are sacred: get to the bottom of them (even if some of them highlight painful truths). And we also need to operate at the most professional level possible.

- *I could have levelled with him.* Actually, I tried this but received a dead-eyed denial, forcing me to back off. But that's because he was emotionally stronger than me. If I'd said it straight: "if this doesn't stop I'll report you" I may have got through. Sure, this may have wrecked our relationship and further endangered me, but the relationship was dead the moment his behaviour, in my view, potentially threatened my career. Fear, of course (and ignorance of the details), stopped me – so I went behind his back, which was a painful and bloody process that damaged my reputation.

- *Or I could have developed a kinder view.* This is the ultimate strategy, although one impossible to achieve when fighting High-FF neural hijackings at every turn. Kindness? To such manipulative swine? Absolutely. Our aim should not be to become like them. Not only is this impossible – we are High-FFs with our default responses hardwired into us – it is also undesirable. Their behaviour towards others is not to be emulated. Instead, we must seek an alternative route through understanding and kindness.

One excellent book dealing with this conundrum is Richard Carlson's rather homely *Don't Sweat the Small Stuff* (1988). Spending most of its pages addressing people problems, the book divides into seemingly-unconnected 300-word (or so) tips for dealing with both big themes and small irritations. Yet the beauty of the book is that these sometimes twee recommendations build into a totally new approach – taking on some of life's greatest barriers.

Perhaps the most important of Carlson's tips for dealing with people is to "develop your compassion". Just as we did with the gunman in the previous chapter, we must put ourselves in their shoes in order to formulate our best response. Even our manipulative boss will face pressures perhaps forcing him or her to behave in a particular way.

In my own case, my rival had found himself in an excruciating personal situation that was clearly having an impact on his behaviour. Even at the time I could see the agonies he faced but showed no empathy because, in my view, he was behaving badly towards me. I felt he was making me pay the price for his circumstances, which led me to condemn him as morally selfish – itself a ridiculous notion (since when was I so pure I could affect moral outrage?).

Understand their weaknesses

If you recognize the difficulties others face you can immediately develop sympathy for them, which – if you are freer than them of such pressures – liberates your responses. You have also garnered your most important piece of intelligence about this person: their weakness. Sun Tzu would be proud, although he would also implore you to act in your long-term interest, which may not involve an instant full-frontal attack.

But what if you are convinced your tormentor has no pressures – that he or she leads a gilded existence? Then you simply haven't looked hard enough, largely because your RAS has been incorrectly tuned. Obsessed by their impact on you, you haven't noticed the manipulator as a person – trying to achieve his or her goals and relieve his or her agonies.

Once you spot these you are immediately looking them in the eye as an equal. In fact, you are more than equals as your behaviour is somewhat better than theirs. You understand them and have compassion for their situation. They think they understand you but are forced to behave poorly due to the pressures upon them.

Another relevant Carlson homily states that we should "see the innocence" in the actions of others. People are people, and "other people do weird things", is Carlson's view. Yet if we are the ones becoming upset by it, we are the ones that need to change or at least "look beyond it".

Of course, there is a danger in this – that we develop the "you're the insecure one" mentality of the motivational converts. This would be a disaster in my opinion. It is unsustainable and easily defeated because it isn't true. *We are the insecure ones*. We are simply trying to develop better responses when our insecurities are triggered.

Developing win:win situations

Once we have true empathy with our tormentors they are no longer our tormentors. At this point we can fight back and win. And if this sounds contradictory, given the empathy we have developed, then that's because we mostly view winning as a zero-sum game. We are taught "I win, you lose" situations from an early age. Certainly, that's how our manipulator would view it. But it doesn't have to be that way. We can seek a win:win.

Developing win:win solutions is one of Stephen Covey's seven habits. Not only are they preferable, they are the only sustainable way for a recovering High-FF to make progress. We are not good at win:lose battles so we should avoid them – instead fighting battles that create advantages for everyone involved.

So by understanding our manipulator we have created a relationship of equals. We can now offer help before it is asked, seek ways for them to achieve their victories, align ourselves with their goals. And then ask the same of them. They'll have little choice but to accept – not least because, deep down, they will also view themselves as good people.

And if this sounds naïve – that our tormentors will simply view our generosity as a weakness and gobble up the advantage, using it as a chance to manipulate us further – then so be it. We will be in a better place mentally than if we nurse grievances and battle back, either openly or through passive–aggressive obstruction. Remember, you have your long-term goals in place and are executing an effective strategy for achieving them. So this is no more than a temporary roadblock, however large it feels. Treat it as one of Tracy's frogs and it'll straighten out your thinking, as well as create the right imagery for putting the issue into perspective.

> **What's Stopping You?** *Bad bosses are usually aggressive, passive or controlling. All are problematic but all can provide opportunities for you to develop strong people skills. Dealing with a manipulative boss is incredibly difficult but one way is to "develop your compassion" – they too will face pressures that are dictating their behaviour and you will be in a better place mentally if you can empathize.*

14

PROGRESS AS AN EMPLOYEE

For those with a high fear of failure goal achievement within a large organization immediately presents difficulties that go way beyond enduring a bad boss. In many ways, dealing with a bad boss is preferable to having no ready excuse for our lack of progress. Without such barriers who or what do we blame as we watch those with high achievement motivation rise to the top?

We blame ourselves, of course, because we are capable of developing strong techniques for making progress within a large (or not so large) organization. If you stop listening to the monkey on your back and instead start looking at the people you work with and the organization you work for – and start aligning yourself with their needs – then headway is assured or, at the very least, you are in the right frame of mind to make progress, or move to an organization where progress is possible.

According to psychotherapist Barton Goldsmith in *Emotional Fitness at Work* (2009), high achievers have many traits in common, including confidence in their abilities and a trust in their instincts. Lifelong students, they are voracious readers pursuing knowledge in diverse areas. They tend to research answers to problems, asking many questions. And they are good at delegation – surrounding themselves with bright, energetic, talented peers, says Goldsmith. Finally, they live their lives according to their inner moral compass: defining, setting and achieving realistic goals.

The last part has been dealt with and the first part – regarding confidence and trust in your instincts – will come with time and the progress possible when small victories start to add up. But what about being lifelong students and researching answers to problems? This may well be an area the High-FF has neglected, perhaps because we perceive that the organization we work for is not deserving of our intellectual commitment.

This may be true, which means we should find an organization that is. Indeed, one of the first decisions you have to make when starting on the road to goal achievement is whether you are in the right organization. Are you standing at the bottom of the right ladder, as Stephen Covey would put it? If your conclusion is that you are on the wrong ladder, then your early Box 3 research should be focused on finding the right organization as well as on calculating how to get in the door.

Understand the organization

But what if you *are* in the right place? Then your research should be on that organization. What's stopping you from understanding the history and current structure of the company or organization you work for? It is almost certainly all available to read. You should be interested in the chief executive and the other senior managers – wanting to know their backgrounds and experiences. Not only will it make fascinating reading – as anything immediately relevant to us should – it offers a strong insight into where the organization has come from and where it is heading.

However, you should widen your interest from just the organization. What about your sector? Every industry sector has its own history with its own pioneers and celebrities. You should find out about them and be interested in their views. Also, who are your rivals and peers within the sector and how do they operate? What are *their* histories? Which organization is *the* organization for the sector? How did they get there? Meanwhile, who's in crisis? And where does your organization stand in such a league table?

All sectors will have specialist magazines that can help you, although you should use publications like textbooks – taking notes and revising the information – rather than as something to browse and forget.

And if you read the above and think: "you know what, I just can't be bothered to find out about the history of the Birmingham widget industry and its rivals in Germany and China. I'd rather read my motorcycle maintenance magazine" then you might just have answered the question about whether you are at the foot of the right ladder, as well as what ladder might be the one to seek out.

When opportunity knocks, open the door

All this research should give you strong ammunition to strike when opportunity knocks, usually in the form of the office crisis. As Goldsmith says, the office problem – as well as its big brother, the office crisis – is a major opportunity moment for any worker. Suddenly we are in the right place at the right time – on hand with the hose to douse the flames. Yet we must know that it's the hose we need, and be able to handle it. Otherwise we are a long way from being in the right place at the right time. We are simply in the way.

Having said this, not all of the problems are of the *"fire, fire!"* sort. Many are positive moments of opportunity for the organization: how best to market a new product, or take advantage of a crisis at a rival firm, or deal with your line manager's new post-promotion responsibilities.

Become the boss's adviser

In *Why Should the Boss Listen to You* (2008), strategic adviser James Lukaszewski sets out the traits required to get ourselves on the fastest known conveyor to goal achievement within any organization – to be the CEO's (or anyone senior's) trusted adviser.

"What matters to leaders is success," writes Lukaszewski. "They will pay attention to you if they think you have a good sense of what they need to achieve that success."

To succeed as an adviser to the senior executives, says Lukaszewski, you must get involved in projects that appeal to them – providing solid ideas as well as small suggestions. You must not be selfish. Your aim should be to aid their needs rather than nakedly advance your own. Yet you must be curious – identifying, investigating and mastering new and perhaps misunderstood information. And you must keep your ego in check.

Key steps to winning the boss's ear, according to Lukaszewski, include:

- *Being trustworthy* – unless executives know you are onside, can keep secrets and have sound judgement, they are unlikely to turn to you for help.
- *Becoming a verbal visionary* – words are a CEO's "stock in trade" so use language that creates visions and inspires (and be proud when they adopt it as their own).
- *Developing a management perspective* – situations look very different to a boss looking down upon the shopfloor. You need to show the CEO you understand this and can adapt your viewpoint.
- *Being a window to tomorrow* – focus on the future of the company, what you can do today to build tomorrow.
- *Advising constructively* – the phrase "constructive criticism" is an oxymoron for Lukaszewski as negative comments will stop the person listening (and the CEO may turn elsewhere for advice). You need to recast criticism in positive, helpful terms so you are heard (this may take practice). Certainly, when a senior seeks your opinion, it is most usually no more than an invitation to agree, no matter how it is worded.

High-FFs and delegation

Delegation is another key requirement for progress, and is another one of those traumatic areas for those with a high fear of failure, especially when in a junior role. Many junior High-FFs fear delegating because they are suspicious of the motives involved – both of your boss who has instructed you to delegate, perhaps to undermine you, and of your colleague, who may seem overly keen to learn your job and take over. You may also fail to see training others as your role. You have a full workload and are unlikely to be assessed on how well you "make ourselves redundant" (to use the unhelpful phrase adopted by one of my seniors).

So what are we to do? Our best, that's what.

It's massively self-defeating to assume the worst. If it's true, it'll happen anyway. Perhaps being outmanoeuvred and "let go" is just what we need at this stage. We have our long-term goals in place and we were clearly on the wrong path or, at the very least, working for the wrong boss or organization. Yet by assuming it is true and behaving accordingly it is, yet again, self-fulfilling.

And by effectively delegating to others you are showing confidence in yourself, as well as freeing up your time for more important work, although you mustn't make the common mistake of retaining the grunt work while delegating the more creative and exciting stuff because the results are less certain or "it'll save time". Being able to delegate means you've done your time on the grunt work and you're on your way up, so if you hand over the creative stuff you've just anchored yourself to the floor while sending your colleague up the ladder.

Commit to the organization

One thing we must do is commit to the organization we work for or find one we can commit to and do whatever it takes to get in the door. This could include initially doing the wrong job for the right organization. In the bank, for instance, I noticed that many of the female executives had started as PAs and many men and women had joined at 16 as lowly branch cashiers. And my first post-university job was selling classified ads for *The Independent*, simply because I wanted to work on a national newspaper.

I hated the work less than I thought – in fact, I was surprisingly good at it (and have used the sales training ever since) – and meanwhile looked for editorial opportunities, despite being told such a move was impossible. These came in the form of articles on the environment for the youth section and, soon enough, a full-time opening came, although with a much reduced salary and the requirement to learn some editorial production skills (which I have also used ever since). Whatever the compromises, it was a great thrill to win my first ever payslip as a journalist, finally feeling that I was at the foot of the right ladder.

Yet I still gave everything to the classified ads job in an attempt to enhance my reputation within the organization – knowing that being judged well was crucial, no matter what the task. According to management academic Charles E. Watson in *What Smart People Do When Dumb Things Happen at Work* (1999) superior performers put service to others before self-interest, especially as – according to Watson – every organization is constantly involved in a weeding-out process, continually separating those who produce meaningful results from those who simply go through the motions.

To avoid such a fate you should, according to Watson:

- Seek and understand the big picture behind your projects and be motivated by that big picture.
- Focus on the work, not the rewards it may bring (this includes money).
- Live by your word – promoting trust in you.
- Keep your commitments and meet your deadlines, even if you incur costs (in time or money).

Of course, throughout this you should stay laser-focused on the short- and medium-term goals that help you meet your long-term objectives. Judge every task, every meeting, every project, every evaluation, every interaction – and definitely every day – on the basis of whether you are moving towards your objectives. Yet be flexible. You have 10 years to meet your ultimate goals so a compromise today may position you well for tomorrow, while intransigence may set you back years.

"Thank God it's today"

Richard Carlson is also very relevant in coping with the work environment – so relevant he wrote a specific book on it entitled *Don't Sweat the Small Stuff at Work* (1998). Key homilies include "never, ever backstab", "remember to appreciate the people you work with", "ease off your ego", "don't sweat the demanding boss", "learn to say no without guilt", "strengthen your presence", "make friends with the receptionists" and "don't let negative coworkers get you down" – all of which make total sense without much need for additional thought.

One – called "join my new club: *TGIT*" – perhaps requires further explanation. This is an attack on two sorts of worker: the *Thank God it's Friday* gang that live for the weekend, hate Mondays and are likely to have empty work lives; and the *Thank God it's Monday* gang that have no life but their work, hate the weekends and consider the "demands" of their family or friends an intrusion.

"Needless to say," says Carlson. "Members of both clubs think the members of the other club are completely nuts!"

He invites us to join the *Thank God it's Today* club in which we bask in the uniqueness and beauty of each day of the week.

"As simple as it seems, the desire to maintain a membership in this club can make a substantial difference in the attitude you carry with you to work and in fact all life," says Carlson.

A final Carlson recommendation worth noting is to "make the best of your non-creative position", which suggests you have a choice regarding any job you may consider something of a drudge. You can dread the tasks, or you can decide to enjoy them and make best use of them.

He used two bricklayers as an example – one resentfully piling bricks on top of each other "in the hot sun" while the other marvelling at the "beautiful structures" he was creating. It reminded me of the Detroit car workers who used the mind-numbing hours on the production line to invent and test the tunes and lyrics that became the Motown sound – proving that even the most *soul-*destroying work is anything but if we adopt the right attitude.

What's Stopping You? *Commit to the organization you work for or find one you can commit to and do what it takes to get in the door – even if initially doing the wrong job. The best route for advancement in any organization is to become the trusted adviser to the senior management.*

15

NETWORKING AND INTERVIEWS

No matter how hard you try, at some point you may have to accept that you are in the wrong organization. At the foot of the wrong ladder. What then? As stated, doing the wrong job in the right building is a good start – but how do we get even that far?

A crucial requirement for anyone seeking to make progress both within and beyond their own organization will be to develop a good network of contacts. Networking is one of those aspects of work life that tend to make non-ambitious or anti-business people cringe. Yet far from hating networking, many disparagers actually fear it.

This is probably based on their success or otherwise when dealing with their peers in the playground – the place where the concept of networks and hierarchies among peers first arises. Certainly, I had playground exclusion issues: I just wasn't big or tough enough to make the top gang. These feelings were compounded at university, where I wasn't cool enough, and compounded as a young graduate in the media industry, where I didn't seem to be posh enough. But while all these groups and hierarchies are true, they are nearly all based on childish or youthful notions of elitism that are unsophisticated at best and, in the modern workplace, completely inappropriate if not rather pathetic.

Forget playground experiences

As grown ups we should simply forget all those past experiences. Networking in the work environment may look and feel like the playground but it's actually the opposite. We are dealing with an entirely different group of people incentivized in an entirely different way. Tap into what makes people tick in this setting, and we should be away.

While being tough in the playground or cool at university are vital elements for success in those environments, because they are based on exclusivity, in the workplace being plugged into the machine is the key need. Everybody needs to know everybody, and those ambitious High-AMs are equally aware of this. Therefore, the very people who may have intimidated us at school and university for their skills at topping hierarchies are now the ones that need to learn a new skill: collaboration.

Being aloof in an organization – at least when you're a junior – makes no sense at all. And very few High-FFs are aloof or arrogant (although plenty are shy, which can be mistaken as such). This means we already have half the skills we need when in any networking situation, as we are approachable – at least when we're not frowning with anger or fear. The other need, of course, is for the confidence to approach others. And it is here where we need help.

Generating rapport

In *Network Your Way to Success* (2002), marketing director John Timperley offers a development plan for connecting us with our peers and, most importantly, creating rapport from those connections.

"Put simply," says Timperley, "if you have the ability to generate rapport with others, you'll be happy and successful; if you don't, you won't. Without rapport in your networking you'll just be going through the motions."

Rapport building sounds like the sort of skill lacked by High-FFs while innately found within those with high achievement motivation – meaning that we'd shy away from most networking opportunities or just stand back and watch while the High-AMs rapport away. But there's no need. This is not the playground. The very fact we are in the building or at this particular event means, in some way or other, we are a cog in the machine. And most people worth talking to want to know how the machine works and who the cogs are – giving you the chance to introduce yourself by explaining who you are and what role you play.

Of course, some may not be interested in how the machine works and blank or even belittle you. But that's just them declaring themselves out of the game. Most are embittered High-FFs not wanting to change: seeing everyone else as a threat and hating the very machine that feeds them, or being over-protective of their own tiny enclave. You just need to move on and thank heavens you have avoided such a fate or stay and try and engage anyway – avoiding becoming the preaching motivational convert, of course.

Networking potential

Networking opportunities are many and varied and we should be constantly alive to their potential in any situation. In an office this includes our immediate desk environment, as well as on the introductory tour around our department. It can also include real or manufactured reasons for visiting other departments, loo and water-cooler breaks (and door huddles if we smoke), meeting room events, or requirements to visit the management suite. All can deliver results. And remember Carlson's plea to "make friends with receptionists" as well as other support staff. A surprising number of support staff have the ear of seniors and most are gatekeepers of one sort or another.

And for both employees, as well as those freelancing or working alone, researching and attending networking events is an important requirement. At work, lobbying to attend such events shows commitment, enthusiasm and a willingness to learn. Indeed, for everyone, such events link us into our sector more effectively than just about any other route.

Timperley has some strong tips for developing good rapport with others at such an event, and elsewhere. You should (with added thoughts of my own):

- *Smile* – however forced, it is better than a frown in making you approachable. You should practice your smile in front of the mirror, making sure it lights up your face to the point where it looks like you mean it.
- *Put them in the spotlight* – be interested in who you meet. Who cares whether you have got your vital points across? In fact, by listening you have – you have informed them you are interested in them, which is crucial for good networking. In *What They Don't Teach You at Harvard Business School*, Mark McCormack writes that the ability to listen, and to "really hear what someone is saying" has greater business implications than simply "gaining insight" into people. He cites Pepsi wrestling the Burger King account from Coke only once they started properly listening to the client.
- *Mirroring* – broadly mirror the person's body language, although not to the point of freaking them out. You don't need the NLPer's intensity in this but, by adopting the same general posture, speed of speech, arm placement – that sort of thing – you can build unconscious rapport. Certainly, body language is vital when you first meet new people. According to Mark McCormack, people are constantly revealing themselves through conscious (e.g. dress) or unconscious (e.g. body language) signals. But this is a two-way street, meaning you should both observe and signal.
- *Dress to impress* – forget attempts at individualism and adopt "group norms" says Timperley. And in the world of work this means dress. While different sectors have different uniforms,

most office work involves the standard office attire (either suits or smart casual). And for men that also means being clean-shaven, avoiding wacky piercings, tattoos, jewellery or hair products. Female uniforms are more subtle but are still worth noting and observing. The way female executives dress, for instance, is usually very different to that of PAs and reception-ists. And the clothes you wear to work should look like they are meant for work – not for impressing potential conquests in a nightclub. Of course, creative industries have trendier uni-forms – perhaps including piercings, tattoos and facial hair. But, even here, understating your appearance – at least until you are established – is better than an outrageous affectation that, if you shoot wide, could undermine rather than build your confidence.

- *Seek to understand and seek to empathize* – no matter what they are saying and how far it may diverge from your own perspective, you are not there to argue but to win people over. As Richard Carlson says, no matter what their view, you should agree with them – "just for fun".

- *Use names* – Timperley cites Dale Carnegie's line that a person's name is the "sweetest sound anyone ever hears", so you should make efforts to remember people's names. One trick I was taught in sales training was to repeat back someone's name immediately as we are introduced. "Hi, I'm Daphne," she says. "Hello Daphne, how are you?" we say back. Of course, we may have to say Daphne a few times for it to lodge and we shouldn't use it so often it unnerves them.

- *Make contacts feel special* – this works across the board when dealing with people. As High-FFs we are so inwardly focused – so often wrapped up in our own feelings of insecurity – that we forget that the most effective thing we can do in any people situation is to make the other person feel like the valued one. Pay subtle compliments – it's the best sales tool known to man.

- *Introduce yourself well* – practise a good intro. For instance, if you say something like: "Hi – I'm the boring one you won't want to talk to" you'll quickly prove yourself right. Don't lie, of course, but focus on the positive, or make a joke. "Hi – I've just started in waste management – boy, is that sector in need of a clean up!" OK, maybe not that one.

- *Be warm* – Timperley states that your opening line can be virtually anything as long as it is delivered warmly and puts people at their ease.

- *Shake hands* – in most situations it is polite to offer a handshake, but take note of the norms in the room. Avoid the *"moaw, moaw"* kissing unless it is *de rigueur* in your industry, and even then don't over assume – it is often intended as a greeting for insiders. And those handshakes – every book I read insists on a firm handshake, so I will do the opposite and warn against the bone-crusher. A gentle squeeze is fine – too firm and you can come across as a rooky salesman.

- *Use space effectively* – this is a difficult one for me as I suffer a bit from cocktail party syndrome, which means that noisy situations make hearing difficult. I try to stand back but lean in, which – of course – has the added benefit of projecting attentiveness. Otherwise, Timperley offers the insight that standing next to someone facing the same way but with aligned body-language can be both informal and "sharing" and is better than the more adversarial face-to-face.

- *Reveal yourself* – all that listening means you should offer something of yourself, or they may feel interrogated. Be open, you have nothing to hide. I have also found the line "I'm new and keen to build up my network of contacts in the industry" a disarming gambit that often has people keen to prove they are a worthy contact.

Networking don'ts

And there are some clear "don'ts" when it comes to both networking and office behaviour generally, of which number one is "don't mix sex and networking". Being overly flirty changes the dynamic of a conversation, alienates everyone else in the group, is unprofessional and destroys reputations faster than any other trait bar theft or violence. Even if it appears to be initially successful, by using the prospect of sex as a means of advancement you are announcing that you have no other skills worth considering and should be judged as such.

Success by this route means being disliked and disrespected by your colleagues at all levels, which will ultimately place limits on your prospects. Let the cocky High-AMs trip up on this one. We High-FFs should watch, learn and avoid.

For other "don'ts" we should turn to Dale Carnegie's famous tome *How to Win Friends and Influence People*, originally published in the 1930s.

"Criticisms are like homing pigeons, they always return home," writes Carnegie.

Being nice about people was his first and most important principle. And it is especially true when networking. I have made some terrible gaffes by trying to be interesting and funny and sounding like an insider by repeating some gossip or criticism I heard about an industry name or even just repeating an unflattering nickname – only for it to get back to them and for two contacts and my reputation to be damaged.

Bitching is a High-FF trait based on our own insecurities. It is also one we should actively suppress.

"Any fool can criticize, condemn and complain," says Carnegie, "and most fools do. But it takes character and self-control to be understanding and forgiving."

Carnegie also implores us to avoid arguments, show respect, see the other's point of view, begin in a friendly way (even if angry) and to try and get a "yes" at the beginning of a conversation – any yes.

Yet all this networking needs to have some impact, doesn't it? Well no. As long as we are on the right ladder knowing other industry insiders is a dividend in itself. Networks are like ripples in a lake, each fanning out to hit every shore at some point. Sales, jobs, partnerships, staff, publicity – all may come to you from some distant shore at some distant date, thanks to the ripples started from one conversation.

Should any openings come up . . .

But contacts are pebbles thrown in the lake, not rocks. You should therefore temper your expectations. If you want them to offer you a job you may need to throw rocks – i.e. directly state your intentions to those you want to work for (although never do this at a networking event).

Your rocks, however, should be well targeted. You should actively research the organization you want to work for, source the right person and focus your attention on that person. But, again, you should temper your expectations – just offering a polite note that, while your current employment is fruitful, your ultimate aim is to join the leading/most innovative/largest or whatever organization in the sector and, should any openings come up in the foreseeable future . . .

Avoid desperation, over-baking the cake, pompous jargon or sycophancy. This is simply one professional communicating to another about their preferred intentions. And avoid being seen as a runaway. As an employer I now ask every person I interview whether they are simply running away from their current job. Like philanderers, and some murderers, runaways tend to encourage the prefix "serial".

Dealing with interviews

Yet this process involves another major hurdle for those with a high fear of failure: interviews. And interviews. And interviews. To become a banker I had to endure three informal meetings, four formal interviews, a dinner, two lunches, two major drinking sessions and a weekend offsite in the Home Counties (and that's not counting the speech at the annual offsite, delivered in both New York and London). And despite my High-FF propensity for exaggeration I'm afraid this is not only true, it is no more than the norm for most key senior appointments in an age when recruitment mistakes can be crippling.

In *Great Answers to Tough Interview Questions* (2001), Martin John Yate (author of the *Knock em' Dead* . . . series of books) states that your aim in interviews should be to offer concrete proof of your suitability based on experience and skills. Even college volunteering or internships can be presented to support the requirements of the post although "an untruth or exaggeration could cost you a job". Certainly, references to thin experience are better than saying you are enthusiastic or a quick learner, both of which are meaningless.

Yate warns that many interview questions are a trap. These include (again with added interpretation):

- *What are your least favourite office chores?* The interviewer is trying to calculate your maturity – rebuff it with positive statements about acquiring valuable skills "even from routine tasks".
- *How did you choose your university?* The interviewer is trying to establish whether you are a stay-at-homer or have some drive.
- *How did you pay for tuition?* Mention any part-time jobs – avoid looking like a "trustafarian" (a UK term for someone with a private income).
- *What were the highs and lows of the last job?* The interviewer is trying to spot the runaways. Be positive about the last job but say this opportunity fits even better and is the next step.
- *Why are you earning so little?* This is perhaps the only enquiry that can be politely thrown back. At my age, experience is more important than money, you can say, but what should I be

earning (although money and benefits chats should wait for the offer)?

In the interview, Yate warns against "constant head bobbing syndrome" – offering the head tilt and occasional slow nod as an alternative, and he is not keen on grinning or hand usage that may give covert signals. These include pen tapping (impatience), hands clasped behind head (smugness), collar tugging (lying) and hands in pockets with thumbs out (aggression). Eye contact is good but don't stare. Mirroring is good but don't freak them out. Taking notes is good (and helps prevent overdoing both the eye contact and mirroring) but don't write verbatim.

In sales training I was taught that the aim of the call was not to get a sale. It was to get the next call. The aim of the second call? To get a meeting. The aim of the meeting? To get a second meeting. The aim of the second meeting? To get the sale by the third meeting. Remember that you are simply trying to get to the next stage – don't rush the process but be grateful if you avoid three informal meetings, four formal interviews, a dinner . . .

What's Stopping You? *Strong networking is essential in any career and is achievable once you understand the dynamics. You are not there to prove yourself but to win people over – so don't expect any immediate dividend. In interviews, even thin experiences are better than meaningless promises.*

16

LEADERSHIP

Leadership is a strange concept for those with high fear of failure. To progress we will almost certainly have to manage people, build teams, give instruction: *lead*. Leadership may be thrust upon us – and must be if we are to progress. Yet, as High-FFs, we have none of the natural faculties of leadership and will, in fact, have a lot of the faculties that suggest we should avoid taking charge of others. Leadership, for the High-FF, can seem like a contradiction in terms.

Yet, like goal achievement, leadership is possible as long as we are prepared to accept who we are – including our faulty wiring – and externalize and depersonalize our experiences. If we can remove our obsession with our immediate selves – by thinking, instead, of the longer-term *Me Inc.* – we can become highly effective leaders.

Simply defined, leadership is goal achievement for a group of individuals. All teams have objectives and, as its leader, you need to be fully on-board with those goals. And if they are *your* goals, then leadership is no more than the recruitment of others in pursuit of them, which is a fantastic turnaround for High-FFs more used to being recruited by those with high achievement motivation to help pursue *their* goals.

Given that you are the guardian and guarantor of your own achievements, you should, first, acquire some leadership skills and, second, lose your fear of exercising them. In fact "exercising" is a good word because we get better at management with practice. I have been managing people in one form or another for 17 years and cringe at some of my earlier fumblings. They were – based on my insecurities and paranoia – tactless, clumsy, selfish, and appallingly instructed and executed. *Sorry!*

Leadership suits the High-FF

Luckily for those around me I am marginally better today, not least because the world is moving the way of the High-FF when it comes to leadership. According to corporate transformation expert Manfred Kets de Vries in *The Leadership Mystique* (2001), business leaders have traditionally been trained to focus on "hard data and cold logic". "Soft" matters such as emotion and intuition are considered immeasurable in terms of output so, in management terms, irrelevant. And, indeed, emotional issues tend to be underlying and difficult to see, and therefore especially difficult to manage.

Yet ignoring soft matters can harm your prospects as a leader, says Kets de Vries.

"Emotional intelligence plays a vital role in the leadership equation," he says. "It comes down to this: people who are emotionally intelligent are more likely to be effective as leaders."

This takes us right back to Daniel Goleman's book *Emotional Intelligence* and his focus on EQ. Yet by the time we have moved up the ladder to the point of leading a team, things have moved in the High-FF's favour, especially in the modern world. Most people reading this book will work in the knowledge economy. This is the world of the office or studio and it involves people who possess both skills and choices. We are a long way from the industrialized workforce of the last century, with workers undertaking fractional and brainless tasks and productivity measured purely in quantitative output.

Productivity in the modern economy involves qualitative measurements such as creativity, thought leadership, analysis and mental processing. And this requires humans who are emotionally as well as intellectually capable of performing such tasks. It also requires leaders who can motivate workers through emotional awareness and intelligence.

A new approach to leadership

As Kets de Vries puts it, the old leadership model of "command, control and compliance" has been replaced by the new model of "ideas, information and interaction". The old paternal model of lifetime employment and lifetime loyalty has been replaced by a more adult relationship, which is a major revolution in management needs and one that – surprisingly – plays right into our hands as recovering High-FFs.

But we must learn how to capitalize upon it. Our self-obsession may prevent us from seeing that, as High-FFs, our previous weaknesses – of being too emotional, too sensitive, of being overly concerned with not losing face, of giving too much credence to external opinions – become our strengths. Yet, to lead, we must externalize these experiences and see it from the viewpoint of others, especially those we lead.

Certainly, High-FF leadership seems counterintuitive until we step through the mirror. Once through, our experiences – if we can learn from them – give us a strong understanding of the needs of the people we lead. The experiences of those with high achievement motivation, however, render them clueless.

The crucial ability: empathy

In *Working with Emotional Intelligence*, the 1998 follow-up to *Emotional Intelligence*, Daniel Goleman states that our ability to empathize with the emotional needs of others is crucial in the modern world of work – an essential building block in business leadership that underpins our ability to be a mentor and to navigate sometimes conflicting workplace personalities.

Optimal productivity requires strong interpersonal relationships, he says, that we may ruin if we fail to pay enough attention to the emotional impact of our decisions on those we lead. And while this can trip up ambitious High-AMs who are solely focused on achievement motivation, the insecurities we carry as recovering High-FFs should give us an awareness – as well as a sensitivity – of the hierarchy below that should work in our favour as long as we are intelligent enough to realize that the emotions we felt on the way up are the same as those now being felt by our team.

Goleman's key point is that the people we lead are at least as important as the people we follow, despite their lower position in the hierarchy. And this means that – just for once – our insecurities as High-FFs, where we are so often concerned about what people think of us or how we are being perceived, is on-the-money when it comes to leadership. Yet, extraordinarily, this is the very moment, with the very people, that High-FFs can decide to become insensitive. Once in the boss's camp of achievement motivation, many High-FFs feel they should adopt High-AM ways – perhaps by focusing solely on goal achievement rather than on listening to their team – which is a disaster because, in this instance, the High-AM should be adopting the thinking of the High-FF.

The paradox of success

Marshall Goldsmith (with Mark Reiter) addresses this very concern in his book *What Got You Here Won't Get You There* (2008). In what he calls the "paradox of success", Goldsmith explains that the same beliefs and behaviours that made people successful can create problems when they lead.

Ironically, problem behaviours can include:

- "winning too much", which makes them trample over others
- "adding too much value", which prevents others getting any credit
- "passing judgement", which means offering opinions rather than listening
- "being straight talking" which means making destructive comments and being too critical, and
- "telling the world how smart they are", rather than offering praise to others.

These are all traits that those with high achievement motivation have used to get to the top. Now there, however, they can alienate the team below them and destroy confidence, creativity, optimism and, ultimately, loyalty. Little wonder that so many High-AMs, when made the boss, simply keep going: acquiring companies, becoming corporate raiders, throwing themselves into maniacal deal-doing and even becoming crooks. Anything but nurture the team beneath them.

In fact we only need to understand the word "leadership" to see the error. It isn't advanced "followship" up the hierarchy or across to larger peers. It's our ability to inspire the people in the hierarchy below that matters.

One minute management

So how best to achieve this? In my view the single most effective action we can take as a strong leader is to back off. In the *One Minute Manager* (1983), management trainer Ken Blanchard (with Spencer Johnson) sets out to prove that less is more when it comes to team instruction. What happens in those all-important 60 seconds is not instruction or management by the leader but the setting out of an agreed vision regarding the result of a project or task. How they arrive at this result is up to those charged with execution. This leaves the team incentivized to complete the task as best they can. It is *their* task after all, and they should get all the credit.

Blanchard's style of management is aimed at building confidence and a sense of ownership. With such autonomy the leader hasn't simply let go – Blanchard builds in additional elements such as the *One Minute Reprimands* or *One Minute Praisings* if the manager needs to intervene (although the reprimands, at least, should be executed sparingly). Yet by showing such a sense of trust in their team, the leader has unleashed the team's full potential to reward that empowerment.

Make others feel important

But there are also more engaged leadership traits. In *How to Win Friends and Influence People*, Dale Carnegie states that one of the most important traits in any influential person is making other people feel important. No matter how young or inexperienced our team, this is a strong basic desire among all human beings and, as a team leader, we have the power to inject others with that feeling.

Another Carnegie recommendation is to offer praise liberally. This doesn't have to be when undeserved, although even when reprimanding, the management concept of the "sh*t sandwich" is a good one (the idea of first stating what's good, then tackling the problems, before ending on a positive note). Yet praise should be wholehearted and meant, not delivered through gritted teeth.

In my opinion, praise is the second most valuable currency after money – in fact, used wisely, it can go where money can't. For all but the most greedy, money is an avoidance commodity. Most people, especially when young, are avoiding not earning money rather than actively working to accumulate wealth. As stated, what most people seek is a sense of achievement or wellbeing – of being valued as important. And in this respect the currency they value is praise. As a leader you should value the criticism you receive (a difficult task for the High-FF, admittedly) but you should also value the praise that you give: it is far more important than the criticism.

Maslow's hierarchy of needs

If this seems far-fetched then we simply need to refer to Maslow's hierarchy of needs. Abraham Maslow was interested in exemplary people and their motivations, which turned into a theory of human needs and self-actualization. Usually expressed as a pyramid, Maslow in his 1943 paper *A Theory of Human Motivation* states that humans move up from the basic physiological needs for food, water and sleep to require safety in the form of shelter, employment and health. Above that, humans need friendship and love and above that self-esteem, confidence, achievement and respect. And at the very top of the pyramid are attributes such as morality and creativity. At all levels money is simply a means to an end.

This is an enlightening concept for any team leader, and far more powerful than a pay scale – not least because it is apparent that humans cannot graduate up to the next level without satisfying the needs of the lower level. Only once we have food and water can we think about shelter and security. Only once we have safety can we think about love and belonging. Only once we are loved can we think about self-esteem and respect. And only once we have self respect do we crave morality.

Apply this to both yourself and your team and it is apparent that those in most modern offices have moved beyond the safety level. Most, hopefully, will also have well-developed feelings of love and belonging – although this may well be the level where many High-FFs, due to childhood experiences, have become trapped, preventing them moving up to the level of self-esteem and confidence. You cannot offer the love they seek in this respect but you can offer the belonging, which should improve their confidence and desire for achievement, making your team highly motivated. And this, in turn, will reinforce your own sense of belonging as a recovering High-FF.

Generating a sense of security for a team, via autonomy and praise, is therefore far more powerful than operating on a system of fear and rewards: the sack or riches. It is also a lot easier to deliver.

The hiring gambit

But what if you regard your team with such contempt you cannot offer such autonomy? What if they are not worthy of your praise? Well, you may have the wrong team. In fact, this is a likely scenario. High-FFs are notorious for hiring the wrong people. We look for individuals who will not challenge our seemingly tenuous grip on authority – instead hiring people we feel have "the right attitude". We may occasionally fool ourselves into thinking we can handle star players but we will soon convince ourselves – through crises, real or imagined – that we have no room for "prima donnas", especially not ones that seem to threaten our position.

Certainly, one-minute management is impossible without a degree of confidence in our team, so our first task may need to be some strong hiring.

But how should the recovering High-FF recruit? Most "how to hire" books offer reasonably obvious pointers along "tick the box" and "get the regulations right" lines, as if written for HR department rookies. Yet employing someone – especially for the first time – is a key moment for anyone seeking achievement motivation. And we have to have the courage of our convictions here and build a team that will help us achieve our goals. In his seminar-turned-book *Crazy Times Call for Crazy Organizations*, Tom Peters writes with regards to company recruitment (and much else besides): "Most organizations bore me stiff."

Peters is trying to create the "curious corporation", as – in his way – is Blanchard. Can you create and lead the curious team? The answer is that you must if you are to create an effective team to pursue your goals. Otherwise you will keep hiring personal assistants who, when they discover their station, will resent you and, at best, quit – leaving you back at square one. At worst they will make your most paranoid fantasies self-fulfilling.

Spotting curious people

If we agree with Tom Peters that curious people are the way ahead, how do we spot them and persuade them to join? In fact, this is the easy bit.

"I think that Rule No.1 in the corporate recruiting manual is, 'Thou shalt not hire anyone who has as much as a nanosecond's gap in her or his résumé [CV] between nursery school and now'," says Peters.

Most hirers look for people with the perfect CV – good grades, a good university, strong experience in the right places and no awkward bits that might need an explanation. It is the IBM factor for people ("nobody ever got fired for hiring IBM," is a famous business quote). Yet Peters is saying we may be looking down the wrong end of the telescope. People who have travelled or who have otherwise wayward CVs may be the very people we need. They may even be fellow High-FFs who are also, like us, rattling the cage in frustration. If we can determine that this is not just another job, that they see this as the foot of the right ladder – that they agree with our vision without inwardly rolling their eyes – then, as long as we can inspire and motivate them, we are likely to uncover some gems.

"Hire a few genuine off-the-wall sorts," he says, "collect some weirdos."

What Peters is really saying is that being a paranoid hirer may look safe, but can be costly. And that the odd leap of faith in unconventional people could well be highly rewarding – not least because of the loyalty we can build by taking young, talented but directionless people and giving them a sense of direction: especially a direction – thanks to Blanchard – that they largely forge for themselves. Certainly, this has been my experience at Moorgate.

It won't always work

Yet for every hire that works, there is another that doesn't. In this respect, the recruiter needs to go easy on themselves. People are people and not everyone is going to buy into your vision, no matter what they say at the interview or how strongly we try and incentivize them.

We have our objectives and we should focus on those and those alone. If someone is just not on the same page – after strong and repeated attempts by you to motivate them – then you should both move on, seeing each recruiting failure as a step towards recruiting success.

Having said this, it is right that you see each recruiting failure as *your* failure. It is something you have to learn from. Hiring is a skill you have to hone.

Two common mistakes in my early days:

- *Hiring based on avoiding my last mistake.* So often, I would look for the person that my last recruiting failure wasn't, which was another way of not taking responsibility for my recruiting failures.
- *Looking too much at the cultural fit.* Hiring clones is a quick way to confirm our own prejudices but may also reduce our effectiveness. We need individuals from a range of backgrounds who won't necessarily agree with us or each other. If we are sensitive High-FFs unable to cope with criticism then we will decapitate our team's potential. We need broad shoulders when

hiring and should judge criticism from recruits and juniors by our depersonalized *Me Inc.* objectives.

Inspiring leadership

Listening to your team and acting accordingly inspires loyalty. In fact, "inspire" is an important word because that's what good leaders do – it is their key attribute.

In *The Inspiring Leader* (2009) by leadership executives John H. Zenger, Joseph R. Folkman and Scott K. Edinger the trio point out that the ability to inspire is near the top of any analysis or survey of what people or organizations look for in a leader. They write that inspirational leaders have qualities such as charisma, confidence and vision that can create a hopeful, positive, confident, self actualizing and resilient corporate culture.

Oh dear! Perhaps this is an element of leadership still more suited to those High-AMs after all.

Yet we should suspend such harsh judgements for a moment. Superior leaders – through their actions, behaviours and attitudes – exemplify what they want from others, state the trio. Team individuals imitate a role model, with the leader being the obvious candidate as long as we behave in a way that deserves imitation. The pace of work, the standard of output, the client-facing culture and the norms of office life are therefore dictated by you, the leader, acting as a role model.

"A leader leads by example, whether he intends to or not," they write.

This makes the notion of inspiration more than simply the ability to stand before an army and persuade it to run towards an enemy machine gun – with the leader at the front. It involves setting appropriate standards and propagating profitable behaviour by our own example. How you work and behave in the workplace, therefore – as well as how you deal with others – is as inspiring as any *Henry V*-style entreaties to battle. Indeed, a corporate culture that encourages the army to think of ways of reaching its objective without having to run towards the machine gun would be far more inspiring – especially in the modern world where you are likely to be leading highly-educated graduates or highly-experienced professionals who simply want the freedom to develop their own skills while learning from an inspiring role model.

Motivating a team

Anthony Robbins (1992) states that most companies motivate their employees using negative reinforcements as their core strategy. This basically means fear, which takes us back to the primary motivation of the High-FF: avoidance. Yet recovering High-FF leaders, more than anyone, should understand how debilitating this is for the worker, as well as how short-term and self-defeating for the leader.

The second strategy, according to Robbins, involves financial incentives. He states that this is an excellent idea which is usually appreciated, although he says money as a reward offers diminishing returns, especially with respect to loyalty – as anyone witnessing the rush of resignations on the day the bonuses are paid in the City of London or Wall Street can attest.

"The third and most powerful strategy for motivating people," says Robbins, "is through personal development."

By helping them grow and expand personally – through training and mentoring, through developing their autonomy, through added responsibilities and project management, through bringing them further and further into the strategic and objectives-setting process – you will help your team feel passionate about their jobs and want to contribute more, which is going to make *your* life a whole lot easier.

And if this all feels like a long way from the management you experienced from your own line manager then so much the better. Your role as a leader is not to ape the failed practices of past leaders, but to promote a better way and be in charge of making that better way happen.

Loyalty runs down the hierarchy, not up

In fact, the point of leadership is that the concept of loyalty runs in totally the opposite direction to that which those with a high fear of failure both think and expect (or most have experienced). We need to become an advocate for the people who report to us – standing up for *them*.

Donald P. Ladew in *How to Supervise People* (1998) states that we should intervene on behalf of our team when someone is threatening their ability to do the job and that we must insist any complaint about the team is handled by us – refusing to allow others to bypass our authority. We must also be their source of stability in times of change, as well as their catalyst for self-improvement.

"Great supervisors succeed by leading others to success," he says.

If new to the role Ladew offers some "supervisor basics" such a making yourself known (to the entire team), waiting before making any major changes, and ignoring rumours and gossip. However, you also need to identify the people within your team who make things work, set high goals and be upbeat and positive, although you must accept your role as a supervisor. You don't have to be "one of the gang" nor "be a pal to everyone" in order to get them on your side.

Ladew says: "The way you handle the people you supervise is one of the largest factors in your success of failure as a supervisor" – or, come to that, your success or failure as a recovering High-FF.

What's Stopping You? *Your potential as a leader is enormously strengthened if you can remember that the experiences you felt on the way up are being felt by those you now lead. You should delegate effectively, be a strong mentor and praise liberally. You should also be a bold and imaginative recruiter, despite your High-FF instincts.*

PART FIVE
Me Inc.

17

THE HIGH-FF ENTREPRENEUR

How's this for a question at the back end of the book: could someone with a high fear of failure become an entrepreneur – creating and running his or her own business?

Working for yourself is probably the greatest leap you could make in terms of taking responsibility for your own destiny. It is also the ultimate move in depersonalization – taking *Me Inc.* to its logical conclusion. Yet most High-FFs avoid entrepreneurship not least because so much of the "start your own business" literature suggests that the stereotypical image of a successful entrepreneur is a million miles from the personality of those with a high fear of failure. Take this description from British entrepreneurial guru Mike Southon in his well-known business start-up guide *The Beermat Entrepreneur* (written with Chris West in 2002): "Entrepreneurs are confident. They arc born optimists: they simply know they can do it . . . Entrepreneurs are also charismatic. They inspire people . . . they have optimism to spare which they radiate and instil into others around them . . . Entrepreneurs are ambitious . . . Entrepreneurs are in a hurry . . . Entrepreneurs are also arrogant. They know they are good. At everything . . . Entrepreneurs are also manipulative . . . Entrepreneurs use people."

Southon is not alone. Entrepreneurial consultants and authors Joseph H. Boyett and Jimmie T. Boyett come to a similar conclusion in *The Guru Guide to Entrepreneurship* (2002).

"Successful entrepreneurs are the eternal optimists . . . Successful entrepreneurs are not afraid to make leaps . . . Entrepreneurs respond to the negativism they meet by becoming even more committed to their idea – more convinced they are right."

Virtually all start-up business books conjure the image of an entrepreneur as a swashbuckling risk taker – a confident visionary defying the odds and facing danger with a wink, a whistle and a cheeky grin. Yet these books are of little use to the High-FF because they are focusing on a different audience. Southon is a successful multi-millionaire entrepreneur. And in the passages above he is describing himself (an opinion I can back up from meeting him on several occasions). *The Guru Guide* . . . is similar, citing "natural leaders" willing to make "leaps" including the founders of Microsoft, Netscape, Disney, Home Depot, Ben & Jerry's Ice Cream, Virgin Group, Dell Computers and Amazon to name just a few.

Both books are focused on the giants and wannabe giants – examining them for clues to becoming a trailblazing entrepreneur of the Sam Walton or Richard Branson stripe. Yet in my opinion the vast majority of entrepreneurs are not like that.

The entrepreneurial myth

A better perspective comes from small-business guru Michael Gerber's important book on why most small businesses fail, called *The E-Myth Revisited* (2004). Referring to the "entrepreneurial myth", Gerber states that people start businesses for many reasons but that most businesses are not started by visionary entrepreneurs but by bookkeepers, barbers, plumbers, salespeople and secretaries who grow tired of working for somebody else.

This definitely chimes with those suffering from high fear of failure, as many may have concluded that their greatest barrier to progress is their current boss or the company they work for.

High-FFs may feel that their talents are ignored or there is prejudice against them, making running their own business a practical solution despite their genuine fears.

"Great businesses are not built by extraordinary people but by ordinary people doing extraordinary things," says Gerber.

Another strong book on this subject is *Never Bet the Farm* (2006) by US entrepreneurs Anthony Iaquinto and Stephen Spinelli Jr. They also de-myth the heroic entrepreneur, stating that start-up business people are just ordinary people with fears and faults like everyone else. Indeed, a key proposition of *Never Bet the Farm* is to be realistic, stating that successful entrepreneurs are "risk managers, not risk takers".

"You should never get comfortable with fear, nor should you try to conquer or ignore it," they state – interestingly citing both Wal-Mart's Sam Walton and Virgin's Richard Branson as two among many who overcame fear-related handicaps to achieve their goals.

And closer to home there's Rachel Bridge, *The Sunday Times* Enterprise Editor. Many of her interviews with British entrepreneurs from all walks of life have made it into several books, including *How I Made It* (2005). In the introduction she describes the typical entrepreneur, or rather she doesn't as she states that entrepreneurs come in all shapes and sizes: "they can be old and young, well educated or not, male or female, naturally confident or painfully shy". She also states that they can be the type of person who "dreams up a dozen new business ideas a day or the sort who has only ever had one – which may not even be original".

"What makes the whole idea of becoming a successful entrepreneur so very exciting," she concludes, "is that there are no rules."

My own experience backs this up. At the height of the dotcom boom, I co-founded and became CEO of Metrocube, an "e-business" incubator that leased two no-frills office blocks on the trendy fringes of London's financial district. We installed state-of-the-art technology with the goal of providing space for young dotcom entrepreneurs – getting them out of their bedrooms and into an environment where they could incubate their enterprises.

Ultimately the bubble burst and most of the young enterprises were carried out in a box. Meanwhile, we broadened our scope to include a diverse range of start-ups – meaning that in the three years of our operation we witnessed, and in many cases helped incubate, over 200 small companies.

Traits for sustainability

As CEO I met every one of these companies as they applied to join the community. I also developed a strong sense regarding each company's potential, or otherwise, and charged more or less deposit accordingly. The aim was to create sustainable enterprises capable of steady growth. If that generated an entity of 10 or so people, then that was seen as a great result. Yet – while the sustainable companies were run by people from all backgrounds and with varying personalities – I couldn't help noticing they tended to have certain traits in common. These were my (totally unscientific) observations:

Clarity – the companies that worked had an obvious business plan, usually involving something which was already happening but where they had a niche or an improved method of delivery or execution. Sure, the dotcom craziness made evaluations along these lines more difficult but I still learned to be suspicious when someone couldn't explain it to me in one sentence, or – worse – asked for a flip chart and pen to help me "get my head around it".

Funding – most of the successful companies didn't have any. Virtually all the companies that came through the door showing off about their venture-capital backers with deep pockets were driving at break-neck speed towards a brick wall. They kept talking about "rounds" of funding from ever bigger names, although few materialized. In fact, these were usually the companies demanding an entire floor and then wanting to spend a fortune on partitioning and furniture. Meanwhile, they had no income and were burning through their cash at a breathtaking pace.

Income – the survivors came in many guises but they all had income. Someone, somewhere was paying them for what they did, no matter what the amount. This may seem obvious, but it isn't.

Costs – the successful companies were tight as hell on costs. They hated spending money and would argue me down on every expense. These guys would take the cheapest space we could offer simply to get in the building at minimum expense. They had a survivor's instinct for keeping the costs as low as possible.

Ego – the losers had it in spades. I developed a "bolloxometer" when talking to the CEOs and other cocky seniors. Every time the company seemed to be run by an egomaniac, my bolloxometer started flashing red. These characters were great talkers but had no idea how to nurture a company – and its people – from the ground up. They soon disappeared, usually to something "more scaleable" that they'd "cut me in on" or some other nonsense.

Having said this, egotists are also optimists and virtually every book on starting a business states that optimism is a necessary ingredient, which runs counter to the natural pessimism of the High-FF. Yet, again, I disagree. In a lot of cases blind optimists were the maniacs careering over the cliff while the cautious pessimists were the ones pursuing a well-developed plan that had covered most downsides.

Sales – a surprising number of companies had nobody focused on sales, which – for any small company – is suicide. As CEO of Metrocube, and for Moorgate, I saw and see my key role as sales. If the chief executive is not bringing in clients, he or she is either the office manager, which is an expensive indulgence for a start-up, or no more than a cog in the machine – making themselves vulnerable to the person doing the selling. The exception to this is the consultancy type firms, where the clients are looking for the CEO's expertise, making sales and execution a tough balancing act.

Flexibility – as stated, as Metrocube sailed into the dotcom maelstrom we had to broaden our offering to become an incubator for all start-ups. This worked because the buildings' high-tech spec was starting to attract more than the dotcoms. Yet this need for flexibility also worked for the start-ups that came through our doors. Many began with grand ideas about online exchanges or online retail operations, for instance, and ended up being software providers for major corporations looking to develop their own Internet offering. The CEO usually seemed happy with this – almost relieved – although we noticed the trendier and flakier hangers-on drift off at this point.

Exit – most of the successful companies in Metrocube had one eye on "value realization", such as a trade sale to a larger rival. But there were limits to this. Those convinced they would be "IPOing" in six months or so were invariably talking rubbish. However, I noticed that companies with an exit over the horizon, or at least as a long-term goal, tended to have a more professional set up.

Commitment – finally the biggest determinant of them all. It was difficult to tell from the first meeting but within a few weeks it was pretty clear who was committed and who was just having fun or filling in time before college or the consultancy career. Time in the office was a good sign – with those in before eight the clearest winners. Those strolling in past 10 may as well not have bothered (and after a while few of them did).

Oddly, the opposite was true at the other end of the working day. Those staying late into the evening were often disorganized lifestylers not taking it seriously, while those who meant it were gone by eight at the latest. And the all-nighter brigades were also likely to be a flash in the pan. Pool tables, dart boards, fridges full of beer and loud music always made me nervous – all clues that they were playing at it.

Terror is unavoidable

Sustainable entrepreneuring is, therefore, a long way from the swashbuckling land of heroes often described. It requires hard graft over a long period, strong organizational skills and grounded salesmanship. What it does not require is genius or headless bravery or, importantly, uniquely High-AM traits such as over-confidence or blind optimism. Gerber's *E-Myth* . . . concurs with this view, making this an important book for the recovering High-FF entrepreneur. He states that tales of women and men defying all odds to win fame and profit are rarely true and are a false god for those pondering a start-up business. The real story is the initial spark of entrepreneurial excitement dissolving into "terror, exhaustion and misunderstanding".

Yet such descriptions should not deter the recovering High-FF – far from it. Terror is our natural state. We should be able to cope with it better than those High-AMs who may truly experience fear for the first time once the support mechanisms of a large organization disappear. Certainly, as an entrepreneur I spend my days in a state of fear – especially in December when our annual PR contracts are renewed (or otherwise). But I spent my days as a banker in fear. The difference now is that I'm in control. It's fear with the frustration removed. And that is the fear of freedom, which tastes a whole lot sweeter.

> **What's Stopping You?** *There is no such thing as a "typical" entrepreneur so don't be put off by the image. All you need is a strong desire to work for yourself, commitment and organization. Yes, you will experience fear, but fear as an entrepreneur is the fear of freedom, which tastes a lot sweeter.*

FUNDING, BOOTSTRAPPING AND PARTNERSHIPS

O f the traits for entrepreneurial sustainability I described in the previous chapter, one will strike many as counter-intuitive: funding. Virtually all of the "let's start a business" literature – often handed out for free by banks or grants authorities – will state that new enterprises must be well funded. Of course, money is the oxygen of any enterprise and running out of it is an obvious calamity, especially for the High-FF who may be mentally trying to sabotage themselves from the start. Yet the "strong backing" mantra repeated by most small-business advisors may lead many High-FF small or new business owners into what could be an equally painful fate: the python-like grip of the venture capitalist.

On this I agree with Mike Southon. In *The Beermat Entrepreneur* he describes his own experience:

"At The Instruction Set [the company he sold to make his millions], we built a 150-person company without any substantial outside funding. I recommend you do the same, partly because external funding is a nightmare, but mainly because refusing to rely on it imposes a financial and sales discipline on the business that is very, very healthy."

Of course, Southon states that exceptions exist (bio-tech companies, for instance, that need to fund research) but for the vast majority of start-ups – and especially those run by recovering

High-FFs – avoiding VC money is the best course. Those using their own money are more committed. The founders are staking everything – perhaps even their homes – to make this work, so no one can accuse them of dabbling or filling in time before their real career starts. Sure, Gerber's "terror" has increased but terror is a given for a start-up. The last thing any recovering High-FF entrepreneur should do is replace the old boss with an equally demanding and manipulative new boss – otherwise known as the venture capitalist. And even if using the bank's money – via an overdraft or loan – it is money that will have to be repaid, no matter what the outcome.

The point was to free ourselves from such frustrations, not build our own prison and hand the keys to the VC or bank manager.

Ventures with no funding use their own meagre resources far more wisely – making every penny count. They also know that making their venture work is the only way of realizing a return on their investment.

Of course, refusing VC money feels like an immediately-limiting move – especially if we are imposing the stricture of using only our own funds. This raises two points. The first is that this is entrepreneurialism for the recovering High-FF, so the point is to reduce the fear, which VC money – with all its demands – doesn't. So what if this also reduces the pace of growth? As stated throughout this book, there are no great leaps for those with a high fear of failure – only small self-confirming steps. The need is to create sustainable businesses that reinforce our sense of self-esteem, not to take on Sergey Brin and Larry Page at Google.

Raising cash for a venture

The second point is that VC money is by no means the only option, which brings us back to *The Beermat Entrepreneur*. Mike Southon suggests a total of nine ways to raise the required cash for getting a venture off the ground, stated in order of his preference (with my own added thoughts):

First, our own money. He even suggests family money ventures tend to fail. "Easy come, easy go" is Southon's expression, although there are cases where having something to prove (most often to daddy) can generate strong results. Many of the interviewees in Rachel Bridge's *How I Made It* have a strong element of this, whether they were using family money or not. Many, also, have more than a whiff of the High-FF about them – overcoming their fears and insecurities to "make it". There were no celebrities in the book – just 40 normal-seeming Brits who have taken the plunge. In fact, a few made strong statements about using those very fears and insecurities as a spur.

Second, grants. Southon warns against long lead times, while my own view is that grants have the "easy come, easy go" feel of family money. And some companies have the feel of being "grant junkies". I'd personally rather see grants become loans – no matter how soft the terms.

Third, revenue. Southon has the excellent idea of asking for advance payments from key clients, perhaps offering a discount as an incentive. I know of an entrepreneur who purchased an underperforming but well-known magazine by simply approaching the regular advertisers and offering substantial discounts if they agreed to pay for a year upfront to help him take control of the company.

Fourth and *fifth*, Southon talks of approaching someone who has helped mentor us to this point – especially if they are likely to remain a "cornerstone" of our team. Alternatively, the mentor may know a likely investor.

Yet while this is preferable to VC money (see below), we need to be aware of what I would call "VC-lite". A key issue for any external investor – VC, angel or mentor – will be their timeframe for receiving a return on their outlay. While it may be years not months, there will still be a timetable that may not suit someone working to a 10-year (or longer) life-changing horizon.

And perhaps because of my own background – I would place Southon's sixth option above the prospect of mentor money.

Sixth – bank lending. Banks will want personal guarantees and that seems to be that, no matter what the noise and propaganda from internal or external sources. Most people complain about this, including Southon. Yet I'm obviously more inclined to see it from the bank's point of view. Banks at this level have two core roles. One is to find good businesses to lend to. The other is to get the money back – on time – with the agreed interest. And the entire credit approval process for the bank is to establish whether this first function will be supported by the second.

Sorry, but I can sympathize with this. Banks have no other upside (they make little on day-to-day banking) so why are we asking them to take a risk in our venture that we are not prepared to take ourselves? In reality banks are simply setting an "am I committed?" test that – for borrowers unwilling to step up – should provide both the bank and the borrower with food for thought.

Seventh for Southon is the strategic option of payment in advance from a key customer for an equity stake. Yet, as he warns, such money may come with unacceptable restrictions regarding our future activities.

Eighth and *ninth* is VC money – with the lesser option being from business angels of the *Dragons' Den* type. Southon compares VC investment to the story of Dr Faustus who sold his soul to the devil. Initially Faustus had everything he wanted and more, but in the end Old Nick came and took away the doctor's soul, which Southon calls, "the ultimate asset strip".

Of course, business angels (including our foreword writer) are a lesser evil than the full-on venture capitalists – especially if they can also provide mentoring skills. Yet the recovering High-FF must remain acutely aware of the frustrations that led them to this point – especially with respect to our dealings with people. Sourcing funding by trading our autonomy, therefore, may be a high price to pay to reduce our fears, which are, in any case, likely to remain and potentially be heightened if our investors' objectives differ from our own.

The joy of bootstrapping

For me – and for the recovering High-FF going into business – the ultimate form of financing is self-financing. And this should involve my favourite word when it comes to entrepreneurialism: *bootstrapping*. The dictionary definition of bootstrapping is "by one's own efforts", which in practical terms means making our own seed capital go as far as possible for as long as possible.

This is good news as many High-FFs have tendencies towards financial phobia. We fear spending money because our concerns over the future outweigh the feelings of optimism required to go on a credit-fuelled spending spree. Most High-FFs are used to living within their means, which puts us at a tremendous advantage when it comes to starting our own business.

The point of bootstrapping, therefore, is to start small and stay prudent. In his book *Start Small, Finish Big* (2000), Subway sandwich-chain founder Fred DeLuca (written with John P. Hayes) describes how he began with an investment of US$1000 and bootstrapped his way to a fortune, citing Kinko's founder Paul Orfalea as another example.

"Start small," he implores, "it is better than never starting at all."

By starting small, he states, we learn what to do and what not to do.

"Just because it is small doesn't mean the business can't grow," he writes. "And while it is small you will have the time to learn the lessons that are essential to your future success."

This is reinforced by Iaquinto and Spinelli (2006). Indeed, starting with a shoestring operation is their ninth principle (of 15) for entrepreneurs.

Modest beginnings cushion our business against financial losses, they state, while the need to be efficient with money can spark creativity. And if costs are kept low, start-up companies can charge less for their products, meaning they can undercut the competition – an all-important need for a new business.

Partnerships – a significant milestone for the High-FF

Partnerships are another form of entrepreneurial leverage deserving special treatment, not least because they represent a significant milestone for the recovering High-FF capable of mastering them. The thought of running a business as a joint venture with another person as an equal partner is both enticing – our partner could bring some of the entrepreneurial requirements we may still lack (such as confidence, optimism, courage and other traits typical of those with high achievement motivation) – and at the same time terrifying. We are likely to harbour typical High-FF concerns regarding trust.

Certainly, my own experience with partners has been a bad one. So much so that I spent years adopting the typical entrepreneurial mantra that partnerships don't work, which is patently untrue: there have been as many successful companies built through partnership as there have been by single operators, if not more.

Both Metrocube and Moorgate were founded as partnerships, although both barely survived the experience. At Metrocube my partner put in more money (including family money) and it was his initial spark. Neither he nor I managed to get beyond this, which meant that – despite being CEO – I felt constantly undermined, sometimes even humiliated, in front of colleagues. He assumed his greater shareholding (a majority if his friends and family were included) gave him additional authority, and he thought me a little flaky, perhaps assuming I was filling in time between banking and the publication of my book.

Yet the experience was reversed at Moorgate. A journalist and former colleague suggested we team up. Needing a catalyst for my own nascent plans of creating a specialist communications agency for banks, and confirmation from someone with high achievement motivation, I jumped at his offer of a 50:50 partnership, although I provided the majority of the resources – at first using Metrocube as an incubator.

My assumption that he would play my former role of full-time executioner in this venture – while I finalized the sale of Metrocube and potentially dabbled elsewhere – was, however, flawed. We had very different notions of what it took to start a company, with his eventually angering me, as did his work on other projects (ignoring my own activities in this regard).

Typical High-FF partnership failings

Of course, my reaction to both scenarios was typical of someone with a high fear of failure: frustration, followed by distrust, followed by emotional rather than rational responses. With Metrocube I couldn't accept my junior role – denying my lack of experience at starting businesses – and became obstructive and childish. My partner had a strong track record and I should have accepted his wisdom more readily. He was chairman and I was CEO, yet I misunderstood the dynamic in that division of roles (although I suspect I'm not the first) and assumed I made the vast majority of executive decisions.

And, typically, while rejecting his teachings at the time, I applied them with Moorgate, with me this time the seemingly senior partner. Yet I also applied some of the weaker people-management elements – seeing them as now my right – which helped alienate my new partner. Having said this, my biggest mistake with Moorgate was in allowing myself to become involved in a 50:50 joint venture while, at least in my view, the major provider. Only a High-FF would undersell himself or herself at the beginning – based on their insecurities – to then bitterly resent it in the course of the partnership's execution.

Yet my experiences are poor and, probably, self-fulfilling. Partnerships can be a sound way for businesses to grow, especially if the partners can provide different skills. Partnerships are based on trust, however, and – as with my two examples – if the trust is absent or breaks down they can quickly dissolve into feuding and destructive rivalries.

With both my experiences I felt I was let off lightly, mainly because of the people involved (other than me, that is). Looking back I realize it was my High-FF status that was the main cause of the problems in both cases. My weakness at the start of the relationship translated into distrust during it. This caused me to behave in ways that led my partners to distrust me (probably correctly), creating – as is so often the case with the High-FF – a self-fulfilling vortex of destruction.

Towards strong partnering

In his book, *Let's Go into Business Together* (2001), Azriela Jaffe states strong communication as the "platinum rule" for a successful partnership, which of course sounds obvious until we try and put it into practice. In my case, I was so busy trying to get my own points across – inwardly shouting "listen to me, listen to me" – that I had no time or inclination to listen to them.

Not for the first time, Jaffe approaches partnerships as if they are a marriage. He suggests that, like all intimate relationships, partnerships begin with a romantic phase with giant helpings of harmony, compromise and charm. Both partners are trying to look and act in ways the other will find attractive, and the tendency at this stage is to only see the other's attractive qualities. Yet reality inevitably kicks in – perhaps at the first crisis when those warning signals that have been actively ignored start flashing red.

"The honeymoon stage never lasts forever – in marriage or in a business partnership," writes Jaffe. "Power struggles and disenchantment are painful but necessary processes that all intimate relationships pass through."

Jaffe suggests that the romantic phase is the key moment to put in place the foundations for a strong marriage, which include the following (again, with some of my own thoughts thrown in):

Slow down. Don't rush into partnership. Why not "live together before getting married," suggests Jaffe, meaning first working together on a few projects.

Prepare a pre-nuptial. A partnership agreement is essential. It should state each partner's investment in the venture and commitment to it, as well as other commitments that may get in the way.

Account for strengths and weaknesses. The agreement can include the skills and qualities each brings. This is essential in modern (and more mature) partnerships where individuals actively seek partners from different backgrounds (sales and IT being a typical one). This is part of what Jaffe calls the "paradigm shift in partnering" and is a far more effective approach than two mates going into business because they got on well at college and had an idea over their third beer.

Introduce the family. Would you introduce your business partner to your mother? If not, why not? You may have the same problem with potential clients.

Prepare a mission statement. Even if a marriage of two established businesses, a new business is being created and that requires a new business plan and, most importantly, a mission statement. The creation of such a statement may shed light on differing objectives and motivations, and – once agreed – the shared goals should help iron out minor disputes.

When partnerships go wrong

Of course, every element above is aimed at breaking the fall when the inevitable "day of disillusionment" arrives, says Jaffe.

This is a key moment for the High-FF, who may have gone into the partnership naively thinking his or her partner provided the props they lacked. Almost certainly, the disillusioned High-FF will focus on a perceived loss of trust – behaviours and actions by the other that have eroded what was probably an untenable level of trust or emotional investment in the first place.

Jaffe states that, at this point, you will probably focus your energies on getting your partner to change, an approach that will quickly have you in your corners – hurling insults and perhaps destroying any potential for salvation. If you instead try and see it from their point of view, focusing on how *you* can change (at the very least in terms of your approach), and how you can accommodate *their* view, you may see them also soften their stance.

Even if you suspect your partner of dishonesty, you should stay honest. Even if you suspect your partner's motives, you should remain frank about yours. And even if you are consumed with anger, you should stay calm – communicating with your partner the way you expect them to communicate with you (my biggest challenge, for sure).

The positive side of partnerships

But this all seems so negative – as if the best result available is gritted tolerance and stale endeavour. Hotel entrepreneur Jonathan M. Tisch rails against such negativity in his book *The Power of We* (written with Karl Weber in 2004) – stating that partnerships offer a different approach to leadership and a strong reaction to the testosterone-fuelled "titans of industry" approach that, he suggests, most often ends in disaster and disgrace.

"The myth of the go-it-alone business hero is just that – a myth," says Tisch.

To prove this, Tisch widens the definition of partnership to embrace clients, suppliers, social agencies, and even competitors and employees – not least because it transforms our attitude away from the "me first" ethos. Partnerships at all levels should be equal and based on compromise and commitment, says Tisch. Finding reasons not to cooperate is easy, he opines, while finding reasons to cooperate requires creative thought.

Yet this is all very easy to write. For High-FFs at least, such concepts are far more difficult to undertake, especially consistently. Help comes from the great man himself, Stephen Covey, in *The Seven Habits* . . . His sixth habit is "synergize", which he describes as "bringing together a whole that is greater than the sum of the parts". Covey states that synergy is everywhere in nature – even in the way a man and a woman bring a child into the world.

"The essence of synergy is to value differences," says Covey. "To respect them, to build on strengths, to compensate for weaknesses."

Yet being effective depends on trust, which can be difficult if we react defensively, or by being authoritarian or even passive. These are reflexive reactions, says Covey, which – as High-FFs well understand – can be disastrous. We may oppose or we may tolerate, but we do not actively cooperate and, according to Covey, cooperation and communication are the two legs of a successful synergistic relationship.

"The lowest level of communication coming out of low-trust situations would be characterized by defensiveness, protectiveness and, often legalistic language which covers all the bases . . . ," says Covey. "Such communication produces only win:lose or lose:lose [situations]."

For Covey the middle position is respectful communication, which produces compromise that is "honest and genuine". Yet "the creative possibilities are not opened up", meaning that the enormous advantages of the partnership have been muted – creating a low form of win:win. Truly synergistic relationships – that produce "solutions better than any originally proposed" where all parties "genuinely enjoy the creative enterprise" – are produced from positions of sincere trust, says Covey, where we have fully and cooperatively invested in the other party.

Again, my own experiences – where the motivations and objectives of the partners were seemingly at odds with each other, making trust impossible – makes me wonder whether Covey is being naïve here, although he covers this eventuality.

"There are some circumstances in which synergy may not be achievable," he says, before adding that – even in these circumstances – we will benefit from the spirit of sincere trying because it means we avoid a damaging intransigence.

And this means we can walk away with a smile, a shrug and an effective compromise, rather than with further confirmation of our insecurities and fears. Certainly, compromise and spiritual generosity – whatever the physical cost – is a whole lot better than digging trenches while nursing feelings of injustice, although – of course – some High-FFs are programmed to prefer it that way.

What's Stopping You? *When starting a business you should avoid building your own prison and handing the keys to the VC or bank manager. Bootstrapping is the answer; something, as a High-FF, you are likely to be good at. Partnerships may be a challenge if you have issues with trust but synergistic relationships are possible with good communication and cooperation.*

CONCLUSION –
THE POINT OF RECOVERY

This book began with a healthy dose of scepticism towards the self-help industry. And, having stripped it bare of its useful tips and advice, it should conclude the same way. The modern self-help industry is just that: an industry. It has inputs (insecure people like us) and outputs (books and DVDs and lecture tours and surgeries and TV shows and even the odd gizmo). And it has a process: focusing the mind of the input on his or her own happiness and/ or fulfilment and/or potential.

As Stephen Covey points out, it has also changed with the times: moving from a 19th-century focus on character building, in which virtues such as hard work and efficiency were promoted, to a thoroughly modern obsession with quick-fix techniques that "cure" our insecurities (in "under an hour") and bring us instant success, constant happiness and dream fulfilment.

In an age where we want it all *now*, an industry has sprung up to tell us we can instantly have it all – *well, there's a surprise!*

So is my job to tell you that this is impossible? Not really, as even the most avid devourer of the genre is aware of the over-promising of the "dream fulfilment" gurus (although they may still be vulnerable to the promise of a "cure" for their insecurities when, as most psychologists point out, we are hardwired to our inner beliefs). My job has been to try and marry the two – to accept the science, and the monkey as a constant if annoying companion, but to enlist the gurus and gizmos where they are useful for our progress. To try and offer a route for progress despite our inner beliefs – not to offer a rewiring where rewiring is impossible.

In fact, I contend that many of the gurus would quietly accept the charge of over-promising, defending it on those classic grounds that, if we aim high, we'll land higher than if we aim midway, even if we land lower than the stated objective. This is fine for goal-setting, although obviously contradicts many claims regarding constant happiness (constant frustration, more like). But it is absolutely not fine when tackling psychological conditions such as fear of failure. As stated, self-denial – however deeply held and effectively masked – is no cure. It is a delayed reckoning.

Quit obsessing

Yet this is a long way from a depressing conclusion. It is a treatise for acceptance, one that states that I am who I am, and now let's tackle the future. Although even here we have to be careful. Obsessing about anything – the past, the future, us, them – is unhealthy and can steer us down a dark path to nowhere.

Certainly, this is the contention of psychologist Paul Pearsall in his attack on the self-help industry called *The Last Self-Help Book You'll Ever Need* (2005). Self-absorption, says Pearsall, can magnify your problems until they feel unmanageable. Pearsall's contention is that there is "not just one good life" so you should stop looking for it and look for "*a* good life" instead. His view is that discontentment cannot be cured by consumption, even of ideas. As an alternative, he suggests you pursue his "seven attributes" of a healthy personality:

- Be sceptical, especially of books that distil life's wisdom into a few rules.
- Deceiving yourself about others can be in your interest – especially in a marriage.
- Embrace the craziness of your family.

- Workaholism is not bad for you if you are doing what you love.
- Obsessing about health is bad for your health.
- It is impossible to stay young forever, so enjoy the moment.
- Death is just another part of life.

Be self-critical

You cannot have a positive attitude all the time, states Pearsall, who openly questions the idea of clinging to high self-regard no matter what the setback – therefore reducing your ability to be self-critical. Guilt and shame are not always the villains, self-esteem not the only "sacred cow". Doubt, depression, guilt, even shame can spur people to change for the better, he says, while hope and positivity can wrap people so tightly in their future goals that they miss the present moment.

Instead of self-improvement you should choose a different goal, says Pearsall: enjoying your life. You should therefore savour the present – even the bad bits – instead of seeking happiness in the future.

"There isn't anything wrong with being depressed," says Pearsall. "Life and its transitions can be sad. Crying . . . is not being 'dysfunctional'. It's being human."

In defence of melancholy

English professor Eric G. Wilson takes this a stage further in his book *Against Happiness* (2008) in which he defends melancholy as a condition. Few people accept a melancholic mood as a potentially beneficial state of mind and the entire self-help industry seems to be geared towards its banishment. Yet Wilson contends that sadness "sparks grand thought, sublime inspiration and vital creativity", prompting people to "turn away from superficiality and to look deeper into the meaning of things".

"Melancholia is the profane ground out of which springs the sacred," is his rather florid take on it (he is an English professor after all), adding that such lows keep the "mind questing, questioning and alive".

Those that strive for unending happiness, says Wilson, are essentially seeking control. And it is often the lack of control – the feeling of powerlessness – that most concerns the insecure. Yet Wilson quotes philosopher Alan Watts who states that "there is a contradiction in wanting to be perfectly secure in a universe whose very nature is momentariness and fluidity".

Constant happiness is therefore an artificial state, says Wilson, and its pursuit a religion with its own high priests (the motivational gurus) who fuel a hopeless drive to tame a future that is – of course – untameable.

Stephen Covey agrees: "To think we are in control is an illusion," he says in *First Things First* (written in 1994 with Roger and Rebecca Merrill). "It puts us in a position of trying to manage consequences."

Covey's view is that any paradigm based on control – of time, people or consequences – is bound to fail, so it is pointless to base our happiness on such a quest.

Choosing to serve

So what should the recovering High-FF seek – especially once we have mastered (or at least understood) our emotions and set in place long-term objectives and a plan for achieving them? Again, Covey has the answer.

"Choosing to serve becomes the most enlightened habit of all," he writes in *The 8th Habit* (2004).

Don't worry, I'm not about to get all touchy-feely in the final analysis. Covey's very practical advice states that once we stop looking inward and, instead, start looking outward we are on the path to what he calls "enlightenment" but what I would rather call "sustainable recovery". It might just be the case that the most debilitating High-FF trait of all is self-obsession. And that the most effective counter is the exact opposite – a concern for the other person. Covey's eighth habit, therefore, focuses on "finding your voice and helping others find theirs". Voice, in this context, is your "unique personal significance" – the key element of yourself that you can offer others (without becoming the preaching motivational convert, I hasten to add).

I have noticed this at Moorgate. The element of the job that gives me most satisfaction, that has me inwardly punching the air with self confirmation, is in harnessing the latent writing power of our new employees. When writing my first book I discovered in Strand Books (the famous second-hand bookstore in New York) a book that was unknown in the UK called *On Writing Well* by William Zinsser (first published in 1976). His practical guide for writing non-fiction – along with his clarity and sincerity and sheer passion for the subject – not only transformed my own writing but stirred in me a desire to pass on his teachings, and some of my own. I became evangelical about good writing on even the driest of subjects (and, boy, do we deal with some dry subjects at Moorgate!).

Certainly, I measure the success of Moorgate as much by our ability to turn out strong copywriters as by our ability to attract new clients or add more zeroes to the bottom line. For instance, one unhappy worker left with the parting shot that his only regret was not having learned to write so well at Oxford while struggling with his English dissertation. Another satisfied customer, in other words.

Empower others

So why should you empower others to find their voice? Well, Covey suggests you consider the alternatives. You could try to lead through control, although that is rarely satisfactory and a recipe for conflict, as many High-FFs have discovered. Or you could abdicate responsibility when dealing with people, which may well have been your strategy thus far with obviously unsatisfactory results for your progress. The third – and only sustainable – option, according to Covey, is to help others achieve *their* goals, making that a primary concern in *your* endeavours.

You should help others calculate their own long-term objectives and then set about aiding their achievement, opines Covey. If you do this genuinely – meaning that you are not simply recruiting them for your own goal pursuits or trying to neutralize their attack on you – you can create "win:win" empowerment: the idea that your own progress is bound together with the progress of those you encounter, whether this is at work, at home or even in your social life.

This is a fantastically enlightening concept for those with a high fear of failure, in my opinion. Through binding our goals with those of others we have immediately reduced a damaging self-absorption, which puts us in the right frame of mind to radically improve our people skills. We have also unlocked the positive traits that, as we have seen, High-FFs possess in abundance. Our innate creativity and sensitivity, and our strong potential for leadership, can be positively and fearlessly employed because the result is not about us, it's about them. And by depersonalising our pursuits the monkey is sidelined, or at least more easily dismissed, because it has no domain over other people.

So far from turning us into overly-worthy sandal-wearing do-gooders, helping others achieve their goals may prove to be the High-FF's most powerful and liberating tool for recovery.

What's Stopping You? *Obsessing about anything, including ourselves, is unhealthy and can magnify our problems. Helping others achieve their goals is a strong alternative for the recovering High-FF – not least because the monkey has no domain over other people.*

SUMMARY BY DONALD KIRKPATRICK, PSYCHOANALYST

I was delighted to be asked to summarize this work – giving me the opportunity to situate the book, both with respect to the history of ideas, especially in psychoanalysis, and with respect to current trends and decisions in psychological treatment.

Kelsey has identified a personal problem, the fear of failure, and – I think rightly – argues that this has a mass base. Certainly, the current zeitgeist of endless choice and "reaching for success" encourages this, and encourages writers such as Kelsey to tackle it. Yet he actually taps into a rich tradition going back to 5th-century BC Greece.

The people of Plato's Athens were depressed because they had lost sight of what was good for them and were alienated by the pointless life they were leading. Then as now philosophers arose to offer an answer: that they did know what was good for the people. The project was then the injection of those good ideas into the citizenry by means of words – or rhetoric – the effect of which would be that the citizens would stop being depressed as they energetically pursued the good life as prescribed by the philosopher.

Kelsey has taken it a stage further and offered a criticism of this injection – stating that the positive effects of such rhetoric for the citizen are likely to wear off, rendering him or her further confused and potentially more deeply depressed.

Yet this vein of resistance to what Plato would call the "philosopher kings" also has deeply historical roots. Even in 5th-century BC Athens, Gorgias (Encomium of Helen) was profoundly disturbed by what he saw as the introduction of foreign ideas into a body. Is this not always a kind of poisoning or intoxication, he wondered? Socrates follows on: opining that the people of Athens were depressed precisely because they had been poisoned by swallowing someone else's idea of what was good for them.

And this debate has more modern reflections. Consider the "positive hallucination" first explored as hypnotism became formalized in 19th-century Europe. If via hypnotism we introduce a foreign idea into the subject's consciousness ("I am a love god", for example) the foreign idea sets up a forgetting of what one knows ("I am terrified of women") in favour of what someone else knows. The subject then negotiates the object via this "false connection" and wrongly estimates his capacities – in this case rendering the hypnotized subject a clown strutting the stage as a "love god" while we, the audience, snigger as the ones "in the know".

Skip forward 100-odd years and the concept of conditioning ourselves for success remains, as does the notion that success can be established on the back of a self-induced "false-connection". Renata Salecl argues in her excellent new book *Choice* (2010) that in today's abundance we are anxious to choose the right thing. And this often involves electing a temporary "authority" that can tell us what to do. Most often in the secular modern world this authority is the self-help guru or life coach. And Sigmund Freud argues in his *Group Psychology* (1922) that putting anyone in a figure of "authority" opens one up to "suggestion" with ultimately negative consequences for our condition.

It is in this tradition that we can understand the new authorities that are CBT and NLP, with life coaching and other motivational treatise its variants. This is sanctioned "positive hallucination" (or "positive thinking"). If, with Plato, we accept that we do not know what is good for us, and if somehow we were off sick on the day that the "good idea" was handed out, then we can accept this "positive thinking" as a late and implanted alternative. Unfortunately, the clinical evidence is stacking up: successes are temporary and fade away. Meanwhile, core beliefs remain unworked, and re-emerge.

But how does it manifest? In an alternative school of hypnotism that arose in 19th-century France, what was stressed was the negative-hallucination. Here a piece of knowledge is stripped out of the subject's consciousness under hypnotic influence: for instance, "there is no furniture in this room". If instructed to then proceed to close a door in a furnished room, interestingly the subject will avoid the furniture. But when asked why she took such a tortuous route, the subject offers excuses such as "a creaky floorboard" or "I felt a draught" rather than state the obvious truth of the furniture's existence.

This is the result that Kelsey is so alert to in his work. The hypnotist has not reduced the subject's knowledge of the world, instead has simply reduced her knowledge of why she took the route she did. Secondly, and more importantly, is the demonstration that we do not tolerate gaps in our knowledge of the world. Faced with a "not knowing" of the real reasons for what we do, we will compulsively manufacture glosses that create "false connections" between things – clinging to those reasons against logical assaults.

Kelsey's thesis challenges this notion of "collective forgetting" – as encouraged by the modern philosopher kings – in the way that a hypnotist can cause a "forgetting" with a "negative hallucination". He goes on to show how the omission of that particular knowledge ("I fear failure") leads to fictions that we then compulsively elaborate to explain how our world is, and which we then go on to defend.

Kelsey's philosophy is more in the Socratic tradition of pointing to the difficulty – stating that "fear of failure" is a militant and systemic fact that we ignore at our peril. If we are aware that this particular conclusion (of fearing failure) predetermines our actions, then rather than forgetting about it because it is too difficult – via rhetorical devices, or "negative hallucination", or via "conditions of cure" such as NLP that offer "suggestion" and "authority" – we bear it in mind and keep it in our sights, judging each of our actions accordingly.

This may not lead to the glorious outcomes we hoped for, but it will lead us away from false and temporary pursuits that can ultimately underline, rather than undermine, our negative core beliefs. It also offers a strong building block for sustainable treatment by psychoanalysis, based on the underlying structures established by Freud in the 1880s.

Donald Kirkpatrick
Psychoanalyst and founder
London Association for Counselling and Psychoanalysis

BIBLIOGRAPHY

Agness, Lindsey. *Change Your Life with NLP*. Harlow, UK: Prentice Hall Life, 2008.

Allen, David. *Getting Things Done*. New York: Penguin Group (USA), 2001.

Allen, Roger E. and Allen, Stephen D. *Winnie the Pooh on Success*. London: Dutton Signet/Penguin Putnam, 1997.

Arden, Paul. *It's Not How Good You Are It's How Good You Want To Be*. London: Phaidon, 2003.

Atkinson, J. W. and Litwin, G. H. Achievement motive and test anxiety, conceived as a motive to approach success and to avoid failure. Washington DC: *Journal of Abnormal and Social Psychology*, 1960.

Bates, Tony. *Understanding and Overcoming Depression*. Freedom, CA: Crossing Press, 2001.

Bay, Tom and Macpherson, David. *Change Your Attitude*. Franklin Lakes, NJ: Career Press, 1998.

Bayley, Stephen and Mavity, Roger. *Life's a Pitch*. London: Bantam Press, 2007.

Beckett, Samuel. *Nohow On*. New York: Grove Press, 1996.

Belding, Shaun. *Dealing with the Boss from Hell*. London: Kogan Page, 2005.

Bettger, Frank. *How I Raised Myself From Failure to Success in Selling*. Englewood Cliffs, NJ: Prentice Hall, 1947.

Blanchard, Ken. *One-Minute Manager*. London: HarperCollins, 1983.

Bridge, Rachel. *How I Made It*. London: Kogan Page, 2005.

Brown, Judson. S. Problems presented by the concept of acquired drives (1953), reproduced by D. Bindraand J. Stewart (Eds) in *Motivation: Selected Readings*. London: Penguin, 1966.

Brown, Judson S. Gradients of approach and avoidance responses and their relation to level of motivation. Washington DC: *Journal of Comparative and Physiological Psychology*, 1948.

Boyett, Joseph H. and Boyett, Jimmie T. *The Guru Guide to Entrepreneurship*. Hoboken, NJ: John Wiley & Sons Inc., 2000.

Cairo, Jim. *Motivation and Goal-Setting*. Franklin Lakes, NJ: Career Press, 1998.

Carlson, Richard. *Don't Sweat the Small Stuff*. London: Hodder & Stoughton, 1988.

Carlson, Richard. *Don't Sweat the Small Stuff at Work*. London: Hyperion, 1998.

Carnegie, Dale. *How to Win Friends and Influence People*. New York: Simon & Schuster, 1936.

Carnegie, Dale. *How to Stop Worrying and Start Living*. New York: Pocket Books, 1948.

Caunt, John. *Boost Your Self Esteem*. London: Kogan Page, 2003.

Chandler, Steve. *Reinventing Yourself*. Franklin Lakes, NJ: Career Press 1998.

Chandler, Steve. *100 Ways to Motivate Yourself*. Franklin Lakes, NJ: Career Press, 2001.

Charney, Dennis. *Discovering Ourselves: The science of emotion – understanding PTSD*. Washington DC: Library of Congress (website).

Clance, Pauline Rose and Imes, Suzanne. The imposter phenomenon in high achieving women. London: *Psychotherapy Theory, Research and Practice (journal)*, 1978.

Covey, Stephen. *Seven Habits of Highly Effective People*. New York: Simon & Schuster, 1989.

Covey, Stephen. *First Things First*. New York: Simon & Schuster, 1994.

Covey, Stephen. *The 8th Habit*. New York: Simon & Schuster, 2004.

Cox, Allen. *Your Inner CEO*. Franklin Lakes, NJ: Career Press, 2007.

Daniell, Mark. *Elements of Strategy*. Hampshire, UK: Palgrave Macmillan, 2006.

de Botton, Alain. *Status Anxiety*. London: Hamish Hamilton, 2004.

DeLuca, Fred. *Start Small, Finish Big*. New York: Warner Business Books, 2000.

Denning, Stephen. *The Secret Language of Leadership*. San Francisco: Jossey-Bass, 2007.

Dooley, Mike. *Notes from the Universe*. Nashville, TN: Totally Unique Thoughts, 2007.

Dweck, Carol. S and Leggett, Ellen L. A social-cognitive approach to motivation and personality. Washington DC: *Psychological Review*, 1988.

Evans, Dylan. *Emotion: the Science of Sentiment*. Oxford, UK: Oxford University Press, 2001.

Evans, Phil. *Motivation*. London: Methuen & Co Ltd, 1975.

Favaro, Peter. *Anger Management*. Franklin Lakes, NJ: New Page Books, 2005.

Feather, N. T. The relationship of persistence at a task to expectation of success and achievement related motives. Washington, DC: *Journal of Abnormal and Social Psychology*, 1961.

Foster, Jack. *How to Get Ideas*. San Francisco: Berrett-Koehler, 1996.

Freud, Sigmund. *Group Psychology and the Analysis of the Ego*. New York: Boni and Liveright, 1922.

Gerber, Michael. *The E-Myth Revisited*. New York: HarperCollins, 2004.

Gladwell, Malcolm. *Outliers*, New York: Little Brown & Co, 2008

Goldsmith, Barton. *Emotional Fitness at Work*. Franklin Lakes, NJ: Career Press, 2009.

Goldsmith, Marshall with Reiter, Mark. *What Got You Here Won't Get You There*. New York: Hyperion, 2008.

Goleman, Daniel. *Emotional Intelligence*. London: Bloomsbury, 1994.

Goleman, Daniel. *Working with Emotional Intelligence*. London: Bloomsbury, 1998.

Griessman, B. Eugene. *Time Tactics of Very Successful People*. New York: McGraw Hill, 1994.

Harvard Business School. *Strategy*. Cambridge, MA: Harvard Business Essentials, 2005.

Heap, Matthew and Adler, Harry. *Handbook of NLP: A Manual for Professional Communications*. Aldershot, UK: Gower, 2002.

Hill, Napoleon. *Think and Grow Rich*. Meriden, CT: The Ralston Society, 1937.

Iaquinto, Anthony and Spinelli Jr, Stephen. *Never Bet the Farm*. San Francisco: Jossey-Bass, 2006.

Jaffe, Azriela. *Let's Go Into Business Together*. Franklin Lakes, NJ: Career Press, 2001.

James, Oliver. *They F*** You Up*. London: Bloomsbury, 2002.

Jeffers, Susan. *Feel the Fear and Do It Anyway*. New York: Fawcett Columbine, 1987.

Jones, Carol D. *Overcoming Anger*, Holbrook, MA: Adams Media, 2004.

Kaplan, Robert S. and Norton, David P. *The Execution Premium*. Cambridge MA: Harvard Business School Publishing, 2008.

Kelsey, Robert. *The Pursuit of Happiness*. London: Bantam Press, 2000.

Kayes, D. Christopher. *Destructive Goal Pursuit*. New York: Palgrave Macmillan, 2006.

Kets de Vries, Manfred. *The Leadership Mystique*. Harlow, UK: FT Prentice Hall, 2001.

Koch, Richard. *Living the 80/20 Way*. London: Nicholas Brealey Publishing, 2005.

Kranz, Gene. *Failure is Not an Option*. New York: Simon & Schuster, 2001.

Ladew, Donald. P. *How to Supervise People*. Franklin Lakes, NJ: Career Press, 1998.

Lakhani, Dave. *The Power of an Hour*. Hoboken, NJ: John Wiley & Sons Inc., 2006.

Lukaszewski, James. *Why Should the Boss Listen to You?* San Francisco: Jossey-Bass, 2008.

MacKenzie, Alec. *The Time Trap*. New York: McGraw Hill, 1972.

Maslow, Abraham. *A Theory of Human Motivation*. Washington DC: Psychological Review (journal), 1943.

McClelland, David C. and Atkinson, John W. (Eds) *Methods of Measuring Human Motivation: The Achieving Society*. Princeton, NJ: D. Van Nostrand, 1961.

McClelland, David C., Atkinson, John W. et al. *The Achievement Motive*. New York: Irvington Publishers, 1976.

McCormack, Mark. *What They Don't Teach You at Harvard Business School*. London: Profile Books, 1984.

McGraw, Phillip C. *Life Strategies*. New York: Hyperion, 1999.

Meyer, Paul J. *Attitude & Motivation Volume 2 – Attitude is Everything!* Waco, TX: PJM Resources, 2003.

Michaelson, Steven W. *Sun Tzu for Execution.* Holbrook, MA: Adams Media, 2007.

Miller, N. E. Studies of fear as an acquirable drive. Washington, DC: *Journal of Experimental Psychology,* 1948.

Pearsall, Paul. *The Last Self-Help Book You'll Ever Need.* New York: Basic Books, 2005.

Peters, Tom with Waterman, Robert H. Jr. *In Search of Excellence.* London: HarperCollins Business, 1982.

Peters, Tom. *The Seminar: Crazy Times Call for Crazy Organizations.* New York: Vintage Books, 1994.

Pierson, Orville. *Highly Effective Networking.* Franklin Lakes, NJ: Career Press, 2009.

Robbins, Anthony. *Unlimited Power.* London: Simon & Schuster, 1987.

Robbins, Anthony. *Awaken the Giant Within.* New York: Fireside, 1992.

Royal College of Psychiatrists. *Cognitive Behavioural Therapy (CBT).* London: Royal College of Psychiatrists (website), 2001.

Salecl, Renata *Choice (Big Ideas).* London: Profile, 2010.

Schiraldi, Glen R. *The Post-Traumatic Stress Disorder Sourcebook.* Los Angeles: Lowell House, 2000.

Semmelroth, Carl and Smith, Donald E.P. *The Anger Habit.* Naperville, Ill: Sourcebooks, 2000.

Silbiger, Steven. *The 10-Day MBA.* London: Judy Piatkus (Publishers), 1993.

Southon, Mike and West, Chris. *The Beermat Entrepreneur.* London: Prentice Hall Business, 2002.

Starr, Julie. *The Coaching Manual.* Harlow, UK: Pearson Education, 2003.

The Oxford Dictionary of Sports, Science & Medicine. Oxford, UK: Oxford University Press, 2006.

Tichy, Noel M. and Bennis, Warren G. *Judgement,* New York: Portfolio, 2007.

Timperley, John. *Network Your Way to Success.* London: Judy Piatkus (Publishers), 2002.

Tisch, Jonathan M. with Weber, Karl. *The Power of We.* Hoboken, NJ: John Wiley & Sons Inc., 2004.

Tracy, Brian. *Maximum Achievement*. New York: Fireside/Simon & Schuster, 1993.

Tracy, Brian. *Goals!* San Francisco: Berrett-Koehler, 2003.

Tracy, Brian. *Eat That Frog*. London: Hodder Mobius, 2004.

Trout, Jack. *Trout on Strategy*. New York: McGraw Hill, 2004.

Watson, Charles E. *What Smart People do When Dumb Things Happen at Work*. Franklin Lakes, NJ: Career Press, 1999.

Webb Young, James. *A Technique for Producing Ideas*. New York: McGraw Hill, 1965.

Weiner, Bernard. *Human Motivation*. Newbury Park, CA: Sage, 1992.

Wilson, Eric G. *Against Happiness*. New York: Farrar, Straus and Giroux, 2008.

Yate, Martin John. *Great Answers to Tough Interview Questions*. London: Kogan Page, 2001.

Yate, Martin John. *Hiring the Best*. Avon, MA: Adams Media Corp, 2005.

Zenger, John H., Folkman, Joseph R. and Edinger, Scott K. *The Inspiring Leader*. New York: McGraw Hill, 2009.

Zinsser, William. *On Writing Well*. New York: Harper & Row, 1976.

RECOMMENDED READING

Agness, Lindsey. *Change Your Life with NLP*. Harlow, UK: Prentice Hall Life, 2008.

Allen, David. *Getting Things Done*. New York: Penguin Group (USA), 2001.

Bates, Tony. *Understanding and Overcoming Depression*. Freedom, CA: Crossing Press, 2001.

Bay, Tom and Macpherson, David. *Change Your Attitude*. Franklin Lakes, NJ: Career Press, 1998.

Belding, Shaun. *Dealing with the Boss from Hell*. London: Kogan Page, 2005.

Blanchard, Ken. *One-Minute Manager*. London: HarperCollins, 1983.

Bridge, Rachel. *How I Made It*. London: Kogan Page, 2005.

Carlson, Richard. *Don't Sweat the Small Stuff*. London: Hodder & Stoughton, 1988.

Carlson, Richard. *Don't Sweat the Small Stuff at Work*. London: Hyperion, 1998.

Carnegie, Dale. *How to Win Friends and Influence People*. New York: Simon & Schuster, 1936.

Carnegie, Dale. *How to Stop Worrying and Start Living*. New York: Pocket Books, 1948.

Caunt, John. *Boost Your Self Esteem*. London: Kogan Page, 2003.

Chandler, Steve. *100 Ways to Motivate Yourself*. Franklin Lakes, NJ: Career Press, 2001.

Covey, Stephen. *Seven Habits of Highly Effective People*. New York: Simon & Schuster, 1989.

Covey, Stephen. *The 8th Habit*. New York: Simon & Schuster, 2004.

de Botton, Alain. *Status Anxiety*. London: Hamish Hamilton, 2004.

DeLuca, Fred. *Start Small, Finish Big*. New York: Warner Business Books, 2000.

Evans, Dylan. *Emotion: The Science of Sentiment*. Oxford, UK: Oxford University Press, 2001.

Evans, Phil. *Motivation*. London: Methuen & Co Ltd, 1975.

Foster, Jack. *How to Get Ideas*. San Francisco: Berrett-Koehler, 1996.

Gerber, Michael. *The E-Myth Revisited*. New York: HarperCollins, 2004.

Gladwell, Malcolm, *Outliers*. New York: Little Brown & Co, 2008.

Goldsmith, Barton. *Emotional Fitness at Work*. Franklin Lakes, NJ: Career Press, 2009.

Goldsmith, Marshall with Reiter, Mark. *What Got You Here Won't Get You There*. New York: Hyperion, 2007.

Goleman, Daniel. *Emotional Intelligence*. London: Bloomsbury, 1994.

Goleman, Daniel. *Working with Emotional Intelligence*. London: Bloomsbury, 1998.

Griessman, B. Eugene. *Time Tactics of Very Successful People*. New York: McGraw Hill, 1994.

Iaquinto, Anthony and Spinelli Jr, Stephen. *Never Bet the Farm*. San Francisco: Jossey-Bass, 2006.

Jaffe, Azriela. *Let's Go Into Business Together*. Franklin Lakes, NJ: Career Press, 2001.

James, Oliver. *They F*** You Up*. London: Bloomsbury, 2002.

Jones, Carol D. *Overcoming Anger*, Holbrook, MA: Adams Media, 2004.

Kayes, D. Christopher. *Destructive Goal Pursuit*. New York: Palgrave Macmillan, 2006.

Ladew, Donald. P. *How to Supervise People*. Franklin Lakes, NJ: Career Press, 1998.

Lakhani, Dave. *The Power of an Hour*. Hoboken, NJ: John Wiley & Sons Inc., 2006.

Lukaszewski, James. *Why Should the Boss Listen to You?* San Francisco: Jossey-Bass, 2008.

MacKenzie, Alec. *The Time Trap*. New York: McGraw Hill, 1972.

McCormack, Mark. *What They Don't Teach You at Harvard Business School*. London: Profile Books, 1984.

McGraw, Phillip C. *Life Strategies*. New York: Hyperion, 1999.

Michaelson, Steven W. *Sun Tze for Execution*. Holbrook, MA: Adams Media, 2009.

Pearsall, Paul. *The Last Self-Help Book You'll Ever Need*. New York: Basic Books, 2005.

Peters, Tom with Waterman, Robert H. Jr. *In Search of Excellence*. London: HarperCollins Business, 1982.

Peters, Tom. *The Seminar: Crazy Times Call for Crazy Organizations*. New York: Vintage Books, 1994.

Pierson, Orville. *Highly Effective Networking*. Franklin Lakes, NJ: Career Press, 2009.

Robbins, Anthony. *Unlimited Power*. London: Simon & Schuster, 1986.

Robbins, Anthony. *Awaken the Giant Within*. New York: Fireside, 1992

Schiraldi, Glen R. *The Post-Traumatic Stress Disorder Sourcebook*. Los Angeles: Lowell House, 2000.

Semmelroth, Carl and Smith, Donald E. P. *The Anger Habit*. Naperville, Ill: Sourcebooks, 2000.

Southon, Mike and West, Chris. *The Beermat Entrepreneur*. London: Prentice Hall Business, 2002.

Starr, Julie. *The Coaching Manual*. Harlow, UK: Pearson Education, 2002.

Tichy, Noel M. and Bennis, Warren G. *Judgement*, New York: Portfolio, 2007.

Timperley, John. *Network Your Way to Success*. London: Judy Piatkus (Publishers), 2002.

Tisch, Jonathan M. with Weber, Karl. *The Power of We*. Hoboken, NJ: John Wiley& Sons Inc., 2004.

Tracy, Brian. *Maximum Achievement*. New York: Fireside/Simon & Schuster, 1993.

Tracy, Brian. *Goals!* San Francisco: Berrett-Koehler, 2003.

Tracy, Brian. *Eat That Frog*. London: Hodder Mobius, 2004.

Watson, Charles E. *What Smart People Do When Dumb Things Happen at Work*. Franklin Lakes, NJ: Career Press, 1999.

Webb Young, James. *A Technique for Producing Ideas*. New York: McGraw Hill, 1965.

Wilson, Eric G. *Against Happiness*. New York: Farrar, Straus and Giroux, 2008.

Yate, Martin John. *Great Answers to Tough Interview Questions*. London: Kogan Page, 2001.

Zenger, John H., Folkman, Joseph R. and Edinger, Scott K. *The Inspiring Leader*. New York: McGraw Hill, 2009.

ABOUT ROBERT KELSEY

Over a 10-year period, entrepreneur, writer, former City banker and financial journalist Robert Kelsey read scores of self-help books in an effort to overcome the low self-esteem that was driving his debilitating fear of failure. Becoming something of a self-help addict, he found that, while helpful, nearly all the books lacked two vital ingredients. First, was an honesty about the personality traits they were trying to change – indeed their changeability. Second, was a programme for progress that took account of the innate fears, insecurities and flawed thinking of those with a high fear of failure. *WHAT'S STOPPING YOU?* is the result.

INDEX

Index